I Am Going To BE A Dad

The Modern Man's Guide to Pregnancy, Birth, and Baby's First Year

MIKE FATHERMAN

Dedication

To Ella, my incredible wife and partner in this amazing journey of parenthood. Your strength, love, and patience inspire me every day.

To our little one, who has already changed our lives in ways we never imagined. You've made me a father, and for that, I am eternally grateful.

And to all the dads out there - the ones who are nervously awaiting their child's arrival, the ones knee-deep in diapers, and the ones who have been at it for years. Your love, effort, and dedication make the world a better place. This book is for you.

May we all find joy, growth, and endless love in the adventure of fatherhood.

Acknowledgements

This book would not have been possible without the support, wisdom, and encouragement of many incredible individuals.

First and foremost, I want to thank my wife, Ella, for her unwavering support throughout this journey. Your patience, love, and occasional much-needed reality checks were the foundation that made this book possible. You're an amazing partner and an even more incredible mother.

To our little one, who inspired this entire adventure – thank you for teaching me more about love, patience, and the importance of sleep than I ever thought possible.

I owe a debt of gratitude to my editor, Jessica, whose keen eye and insightful feedback transformed my sleep-deprived ramblings into coherent chapters. Your guidance was invaluable.

To Dr. Emily Chen, thank you for lending your expertise and ensuring the medical information in this book is accurate and up-to-date. Your commitment to supporting new parents is truly admirable.

A special thanks to my friend Mark and his family. Mark, your experiences as a new dad were a constant source of inspiration. The honesty with which you shared your journey helped shape many of the stories in this book. To Mia and little Ethan, thank you for opening your home and hearts to me during this process.

To the countless dads who shared their stories, fears, and triumphs – your vulnerability and honesty brought this book to life. Your experiences will undoubtedly help and inspire many future fathers.

I'm grateful to my parents, who showed me what loving, supportive parenting looks like. Dad, your example set the bar high, and I hope I can live up to it.

Finally, to all the partners, family members, and friends who support new dads – your role is crucial and often underappreciated. Thank you for being the unsung heroes in this parenting journey.

This book is a testament to the collective wisdom, experience, and love of all these individuals. Any mistakes or dad jokes of questionable quality are entirely my own.

Why This Book?

"I Am Going to be a Dad" was born out of a genuine need I experienced firsthand. When I discovered I was going to be a father, I was overwhelmed by a mix of excitement and sheer panic. I searched for a comprehensive guide that spoke directly to modern dads-to-be, but came up short. That's when I realized: if I needed this resource, surely other men did too.

This book fills a crucial gap in parenting literature. While there's no shortage of advice for new moms, resources specifically tailored for contemporary fathers are surprisingly scarce. We're part of a generation redefining fatherhood, taking on more active roles in pregnancy, childbirth, and childcare. Yet many of us feel unprepared for this monumental life change.

Here's what you'll gain from this book:

- Practical Knowledge: From understanding pregnancy symptoms to mastering diaper changes, you'll learn the nuts and bolts of baby care.

- Emotional Guidance: We dive deep into the complex emotions of fatherhood, helping you navigate everything from prenatal bonding to postpartum challenges.

- Relationship Insights: Learn how to support your partner and strengthen your relationship amid the chaos of new parenthood.

- Confidence: Armed with knowledge and real-life tips, you'll feel more prepared and self-assured in your new role.

- Community: Through shared experiences and stories, you'll feel connected to a brotherhood of modern dads.

- Work-Life Balance Strategies: Discover how to juggle your career, personal life, and new family responsibilities.

- Self-Care Tools: Because taking care of yourself is crucial to being a great dad.

This book is more than just a manual - it's a companion for your journey into fatherhood. It's the resource I wish I'd had, and now it's here for you. Whether you're a first-time dad or adding to your brood, this book will empower you to embrace fatherhood with confidence, knowledge, and a much-needed sense of humor.

Table of Content

Introduction

The moment I found out I was going to be a dad, I was standing in our small bathroom, staring at a plastic stick with two pink lines. My wife, Ella, was beaming, but I felt like I'd been hit by a truck - a very happy, terrifying truck. In that instant, I realized that despite being a successful 32-year-old with a good job and a stable relationship, I had absolutely no idea how to be a father.

This book was born from that moment of panic, excitement, and sheer wonder. As I embarked on the journey to fatherhood, I found myself hungry for information, desperate for guidance, and surprisingly emotional. I scoured bookstores and the internet, looking for resources that spoke to me as a modern man facing this life-changing event. While I found plenty of clinical information and more than a few jokes about dad bods and diaper duty, I struggled to find a comprehensive guide that addressed the real concerns, questions, and experiences of today's fathers-to-be.

Becoming a dad in the 21st century is a unique experience. We're part of a generation of men who are redefining fatherhood, moving beyond the traditional role of breadwinner and disciplinarian to become active, engaged partners in pregnancy, childbirth, and childcare. We're expected to be present in the delivery room, skilled at diaper changes, and emotionally available to both our partners and our children. It's a tall order, especially when many of us didn't have models for this kind of fatherhood in our own lives.

Yet, this evolution of the paternal role is happening across cultures and communities. From New York to New Delhi, men are embracing a more involved, nurturing approach to fatherhood. We're attending prenatal classes, learning to swaddle, and proudly wearing our babies in carriers. We're having conversations about work-life balance, shared parental leave, and the mental health challenges that can come with new parenthood. This global shift in how we view and practice fatherhood is both exciting and daunting.

That's where this book comes in. "I Am Going to be a Dad: The Modern Man's Guide to Pregnancy, Birth, and Baby's First Year" is the resource I wish I'd had when those two pink lines appeared. It's a comprehensive, honest, and sometimes humorous look at the journey to modern fatherhood, from the moment of conception to your baby's first birthday.

Throughout these pages, we'll navigate the often turbulent waters of pregnancy, demystifying terms like "mucus plug" and "episiotomy" (brace yourself for that one). We'll dive into the nitty-gritty of childbirth preparation, exploring everything from birthing plans to breathing techniques. You'll learn how to be the best possible support person during labor and delivery, whether it's a hospital birth, home birth, or somewhere in between.

But this book doesn't stop at the delivery room. We'll tackle the intense, sleep-deprived newborn phase, offering practical advice on everything from diaper changing and bathing to decoding your baby's cries. We'll explore the delicate art of co-parenting, helping you navigate your new role while supporting your partner. And because becoming a dad doesn't mean losing yourself, we'll also focus on self-care, maintaining your relationships, and balancing work with your new family life.

What sets this book apart is its focus on the emotional journey of fatherhood. We'll delve into the complex feelings that come with impending parenthood - the joy, the fear, the overwhelming sense of responsibility. We'll discuss how to build a bond with your baby, even before birth, and how to nurture that connection in the crucial first year. We'll also address the less-talked-about aspects of new fatherhood, like postpartum depression in dads, changing body image, and shifts in your relationship with your partner.

Throughout the book, you'll find a mix of expert advice, real-life stories from other dads, and practical tips you can put into action immediately. We've consulted with obstetricians, pediatricians, psychologists, and experienced fathers to bring you the most up-to-date and relevant information. But we've also included the kind of on-the-ground wisdom that only comes from lived experience - like how to change a diaper in a poorly-lit room at 3 AM, or the best way to get spit-up out of your favorite shirt.

Each chapter is designed to guide you through a specific phase of the fatherhood journey, from the first trimester to your baby's first steps. You'll find checklists, discussion points to bring up with your partner, and even a few dad jokes to keep things light (because if there's one thing you'll need on this journey, it's a sense of humor).

But this book is more than just a how-to manual. It's an invitation to join a community of modern dads who are redefining what it means to be a father. Throughout these pages, you'll hear from men of different backgrounds, cultures, and experiences, all united by the transformative experience of fatherhood. Their stories will inspire you, make you laugh, and remind you that you're not alone on this journey.

As we embark on this adventure together, I want you to know that it's okay to feel overwhelmed, unprepared, or even scared. Becoming a father is a monumental life change, and it's natural to have a wide range of emotions about it. This book is here to support you through all of those feelings, providing reassurance, practical advice, and a roadmap for the journey ahead.

Remember, there's no one "right" way to be a dad. Your journey will be uniquely yours, shaped by your personality, your relationship, your culture, and your individual circumstances. This book isn't about prescribing a single approach to fatherhood, but rather about empowering you with knowledge, tools, and confidence to find your own path.

As you read, I encourage you to engage actively with the material. Jot down your thoughts, discuss the topics with your partner, and reach out to other dads-to-be. Becoming a father is not a solitary journey - it's one that benefits immensely from connection, support, and shared experiences.

In the coming chapters, we'll laugh together, learn together, and maybe even shed a tear or two (and trust me, that's perfectly okay). We'll celebrate the joys of fatherhood, commiserate over its challenges, and work together to become the best dads we can be. Because at the end of the day, that's what this is all about - being there for our children, supporting our partners, and growing into the role of a lifetime.

So, future dad, are you ready? Take a deep breath, turn the page, and let's begin this incredible journey together. Welcome to fatherhood - it's going to be one hell of a ride.

As we dive into the first chapter, remember this: you've got this. You may not feel ready (spoiler alert: no one ever feels completely ready), but you have within you everything you need to be an amazing father. This book is here to help you unlock that potential, to guide you through the challenges, and to celebrate with you the incredible moments that lie ahead.

From one dad to another, I can tell you that while the journey isn't always easy, it's unquestionably worth it. The sleepless nights, the dirty diapers, the moments of self-doubt - they all fade in comparison to the first time your baby smiles at you, the feeling of tiny fingers wrapped around yours, or the indescribable love that floods your heart when you hold your child.

So, let's get started. The adventure of a lifetime awaits, and you're about to discover strengths, emotions, and joys you never knew you had. Welcome to the club, Dad. You're going to do great.

Chapter 1

Embracing the Journey to Fatherhood

"Fatherhood isn't about being perfect; it's about being present." – Anonymous

The moment those two pink lines appear, or the ultrasound reveals that unmistakable flutter of life, a seismic shift occurs within a man's world. The news of impending fatherhood triggers a cascade of emotions – a complex symphony of joy, fear, anticipation, and even a touch of disbelief. In a heartbeat, you're propelled from the familiar terrain of your pre-fatherhood identity into a realm of newfound responsibilities and uncharted emotional landscapes.

For some, the initial reaction is pure exhilaration. The thrill of creating a life, of perpetuating your lineage, of watching your genes mingle with your partner's to create a unique human being is a feeling like no other. It's a surge of primal instinct, a visceral connection to the circle of life that leaves you breathless with wonder.

But as the initial euphoria subsides, a wave of anxiety often washes over. The weight of responsibility can feel immense. Doubts creep in: "Am I ready for this? Will I be a good father? Can I provide for my child's needs?" The fear of the unknown, of the life-altering changes that lie ahead, can be overwhelming.

And then there's the sheer bewilderment. Let's face it, most men aren't exactly experts on pregnancy, childbirth, or infant care. We may have a vague idea of what to expect, but the reality is often far more messy, unpredictable, and, dare I say, magical than we ever imagined. The learning curve is steep, and the stakes are high.

In the midst of this emotional maelstrom, it's important to remember that you are not alone. Every father, from the dawn of time to the present day, has grappled with these same feelings. It's part of the universal human experience of becoming a parent. And just as fathers before you have found their way, so too will you.

In fact, the role of fathers has undergone a remarkable transformation in recent decades. Gone are the days when dad was merely the breadwinner, relegated to the sidelines of child-rearing. Today, dads are expected to be active participants in every aspect of their children's lives, from changing diapers to coaching soccer games to providing emotional support and guidance.

This shift in societal expectations is a reflection of a broader cultural movement towards gender equality and a recognition of the unique value that fathers bring to the parenting equation. Research has shown that involved fathers have a profound positive impact on their children's development, from boosting cognitive skills and academic achievement to promoting emotional intelligence and healthy relationships.

But with this expanded role comes a new set of challenges. Modern dads are juggling the demands of work, family, and personal life, often with limited resources and support. They are navigating uncharted territory, forging their own path through the wilderness of fatherhood.

So, how can you embrace this journey with confidence and grace? It starts with acknowledging and accepting the complex emotions that come with becoming a dad. It's okay to feel excited, scared, confused, and everything in between. In fact, these emotions are a sign that you care deeply about your role as a father.

The next step is to equip yourself with knowledge and skills. Read books and articles, attend parenting classes, and seek out mentors and role models. Learn about the stages of pregnancy, the basics of infant care, and the developmental milestones your child will reach.

But knowledge alone is not enough. You also need to cultivate a strong support network. Talk to your partner, your friends, your family, and other dads. Share your experiences, ask for help when you need it, and don't be afraid to express your vulnerabilities.

Fatherhood is not a solo endeavor. It's a team sport, and the most successful teams are built on trust, communication, and mutual respect. So, embrace the journey with your partner, lean on your support system, and most importantly, be kind to yourself.

Whether it's the sudden appearance of two pink lines or the mesmerizing dance of a tiny heartbeat on an ultrasound screen, the confirmation of impending fatherhood irrevocably alters your reality. Time seems to slow down, your heart might race, and a million thoughts flood your mind. Disbelief, joy, fear, excitement – it's a whirlwind of emotions, often hitting you all at once. You're not just you anymore; you're a dad-in-the-making, a co-creator of life, a protector of a tiny being you haven't even met yet.

For some men, the news is a shock, a pleasant one, but a shock nonetheless. It might take a few moments, or even days, to fully process the reality of what's happening. You might find yourself staring at the ultrasound picture, a mix of wonder and apprehension swirling within you.

Questions start to bubble up: *"Am I ready for this? What kind of father will I be? How will this change our lives?"*

Others experience an immediate surge of joy, an overwhelming sense of love and anticipation for the little life growing inside their partner. You might find yourself daydreaming about holding your baby, playing with them, and teaching them all the things you love. The future seems bright and full of possibilities.

But even amidst the joy, there's often a hint of fear. The fear of the unknown, the fear of not being good enough, the fear of the immense responsibility that comes with parenthood. It's natural to feel overwhelmed by the magnitude of the change that's about to occur.

And then there's the sheer excitement. The anticipation of the baby's arrival, the joy of watching your partner's belly grow, the thrill of feeling those first kicks – it's a rollercoaster of emotions that's both exhilarating and exhausting.

As you navigate this emotional landscape, it's important to remember that there's no right or wrong way to feel. Some men embrace the news with open arms, while others take a bit longer to adjust. There's no shame in feeling any of the emotions that come up, whether it's joy, fear, or a mix of both.

The key is to acknowledge and accept whatever you're feeling. Talk to your partner, your friends, your family, or even a therapist if needed. Sharing your thoughts and feelings can help you process the news and prepare for the journey ahead.

Remember, this is a shared experience with your partner. Communicate openly and honestly about your hopes, fears, and expectations. This is the time to strengthen your bond and lay the foundation for a strong co-parenting relationship.

As you embrace the change, take some time to reflect on your own childhood and upbringing. What kind of father did you have? What qualities do you want to emulate, and what things would you do differently? Thinking about your own experiences can help you envision the kind of father you want to be.

This is also a good time to start gathering information and resources. Read books and articles about pregnancy, childbirth, and infant care. Attend parenting classes or workshops. Talk to other dads about their experiences. The more you know, the more prepared and confident you'll feel as you embark on this new chapter of your life.

Don't forget to celebrate this exciting time! Take your partner out for a special dinner, plan a babymoon, or simply spend some quality time together, savoring the anticipation of what's to come. This is a precious period in your lives, so make the most of it.

Becoming a father is a transformative journey, filled with ups and downs, twists and turns. There will be moments of pure joy, moments of doubt, and moments of sheer exhaustion. But through it all, remember that you're not alone. Millions of men before you have walked this path and millions more will follow in your footsteps.

So, take a deep breath, embrace the change, and step confidently into the world of fatherhood. It's a wild, wonderful ride, and you're just getting started.

The Modern Dad: Redefining Fatherhood in the 21st Century.

In a world that's constantly evolving, so too is the concept of fatherhood. The image of the distant breadwinner, a figurehead on the periphery of family life, has faded into the annals of history.

Today's father is a hands-on participant, a co-pilot on the exhilarating journey of raising a child. He's not just a provider, but a nurturer, a teacher, a confidant, and a playmate. He changes diapers with the same aplomb as he fixes a leaky faucet, and he reads bedtime stories with the same passion as he tackles a challenging work project.

This modern dad isn't afraid to get his hands dirty, literally and figuratively. He's present in the delivery room, cheering on his partner during labor and sharing in the awe-inspiring moment of birth. He's up in the middle of the night, soothing a colicky baby or offering a comforting cuddle during a nightmare. He's on the floor, building block towers and making silly faces, reveling in the infectious laughter of his child.

But this shift in fatherhood isn't just about changing diapers and playing peek-a-boo. It's about a fundamental redefinition of what it means to be a man and a parent. It's about recognizing that men have an innate capacity for nurturing and caregiving and that these qualities are not only valuable but essential for raising happy, healthy children.

This new paradigm of fatherhood is a reflection of broader societal changes. As women have increasingly entered the workforce and achieved greater equality, men have been given the opportunity to step up and share the responsibilities of parenting. This has led to a more balanced and equitable division of labor within families, benefiting both parents and children.

The rise of the modern dad is also fueled by a growing body of research that highlights the importance of fathers in children's lives. Studies have shown that involved fathers have a significant positive impact on their children's development, from boosting cognitive skills and academic achievement to promoting emotional intelligence and healthy relationships. Children with involved fathers are also less likely to engage in risky behaviors and more likely to succeed in life.

This isn't to say that the modern dad has it all figured out, far from it. In fact, many men find themselves navigating uncharted territory, struggling to balance the demands of work, family, and personal life. They may face internal conflicts about their role as a father, grapple with societal expectations, or feel inadequate in the face of the immense responsibility of raising a child.

But these challenges are not insurmountable. By embracing the evolving role of fatherhood, men can unlock a wealth of untapped potential and discover a deeper sense of purpose and fulfillment. They can build stronger relationships with their partners, forge closer bonds with their children, and create a more harmonious and joyful family life.

So, what does it mean to be a modern dad in the 21st century? It means being present, engaged, and emotionally available to your children. It means sharing in the joys and challenges of parenting, from the sleepless nights to the proud moments of watching your child take their first steps. It means challenging outdated stereotypes and embracing your full potential as a nurturer, a provider, and a role model.

It also means being willing to learn and grow. Fatherhood is a journey, not a destination. It's about constantly adapting to the changing needs of your child and your family. It's about embracing the unexpected and finding joy in the everyday moments.

And above all, it's about loving your child unconditionally and supporting them in every way possible. It's about being the best dad you can be, not because society expects it of you, but because your child deserves it.

So, to all the dads-to-be out there, I say this: embrace the challenge. Embrace the change. Embrace the incredible journey of fatherhood. It's a role that will transform you in ways you never imagined, and it's a gift that will last a lifetime.

Chapter 2

Partnering Through Pregnancy

"A baby fills a place in your heart that you never knew was empty." – Anonymous

The journey through pregnancy isn't a solo endeavor; it's a shared adventure between partners, a symphony of two souls harmonizing as they prepare for the arrival of a new life. As an expectant father, your role in this symphony is not just essential—it's transformative. It's a dance of love, support, and understanding, a melody woven with threads of empathy, communication, and teamwork.

Imagine a typical evening: Your partner is curled up on the couch, her once-flat stomach now a gentle mound. Her face, once flushed with the excitement of the news, now bears the marks of exhaustion.

Morning sickness, fatigue, and hormonal fluctuations have taken their toll. It's in these moments that your role as a supportive partner becomes paramount. A simple gesture, like offering a foot rub or brewing a cup of ginger tea, can speak volumes. It shows that you see her, that you understand the toll pregnancy is taking on her body, and that you're there to help ease the burden.

Physical support goes beyond the occasional massage. As the pregnancy progresses, your partner may need help with everyday tasks, like tying her shoes or reaching for items on high shelves. You can also offer to cook meals, run errands, or simply be a listening ear when she needs to vent her frustrations. Your presence, both physical and emotional, can make a world of difference in her well-being.

But perhaps the most crucial aspect of supporting your partner during pregnancy is emotional support. Pregnancy is a rollercoaster of emotions, and your partner may experience mood swings, anxiety, and even moments of self-doubt. It's your job to be her rock, her safe haven, the person she can turn to without fear of judgment.

This means actively listening to her concerns, validating her feelings, and offering words of encouragement. It means celebrating her milestones, both big and small, and reminding her of her strength and resilience. It means creating a safe space where she can express her fears and insecurities without feeling ashamed or alone.

Emotional support also means being patient and understanding when she's irritable or withdrawn. Hormonal fluctuations can wreak havoc on a woman's emotions, and it's important to remember that it's not personal. Offer her space when she needs it, but let her know that you're there for her when she's ready to talk.

Another crucial aspect of navigating pregnancy as a couple is fostering open and honest communication. This means talking about your hopes, fears, and expectations for the future. It means discussing your roles and responsibilities as parents, both during pregnancy and after the baby arrives.

It's important to remember that you and your partner may not always agree on everything. Disagreements are a natural part of any relationship, but they can be especially challenging during pregnancy when emotions are running high. The key is to approach disagreements with respect and a willingness to compromise.

Take the time to truly listen to your partner's perspective, even if you don't agree with it. Try to understand where she's coming from and what her underlying concerns are. Once you've both had a chance to express yourselves, work together to find a solution that meets both of your needs.

Remember, you're on the same team, and your goal is to create the best possible environment for your growing family.

One final note on partnering through pregnancy: Don't forget to have fun! While pregnancy can be challenging, it's also a time of immense joy and anticipation. Take advantage of this special time to connect with your partner, create lasting memories, and build the foundation for a strong and loving family.

Supporting Your Partner: Understanding the Physical and Emotional Changes.

Pregnancy, often described as a beautiful journey, is a symphony of physical and emotional changes for the woman carrying your child. As the expectant father, understanding this symphony is key to being the supportive partner she needs during this transformative time.

Your partner's body is evolving at an astonishing rate. It's easy to marvel at the growing bump, but remember, it's not just an expanding belly. Her organs are shifting, her ligaments are stretching, and her blood volume is increasing by nearly 50%. Hormones, those tiny chemical messengers, are orchestrating this grand performance, causing everything from morning sickness and food aversions to mood swings and fatigue.

Think of it like this: her body is a construction zone, bustling with activity as it builds a new human being. Just like any construction site, there will be noise, dust, and occasional disruptions. Some days, she might wake up feeling radiant and energized, while others might be filled with nausea, backaches, and a roller coaster of emotions.

One moment, she might be craving pickles and ice cream, the next, she's sobbing over a sentimental commercial. These hormonal fluctuations can be bewildering, even for her. That's where you come in. Your understanding and empathy can be a lifeline during this turbulent time.

A simple "How are you feeling today?" can open the door to a conversation about her physical and emotional state. Listen actively, validate her feelings, and offer reassurance. If she's struggling with morning sickness, whip up a batch of ginger tea or offer to run errands so she can rest. If she's feeling anxious about the changes happening to her body, remind her how beautiful she is and how amazed you are by her strength.

This is also a time to step up your game in the physical support department. Take on more household chores, cook nourishing meals, and offer a comforting massage at the end of a long day. Be proactive in anticipating her needs, whether it's fetching a glass of water or adjusting her pillows.

Note, pregnancy isn't just about the physical changes. Your partner's emotional well-being is equally important. Pregnancy can trigger a wide range of emotions, from excitement and anticipation to anxiety and self-doubt. It's a time of introspection and vulnerability, as she grapples with the monumental task of becoming a mother.

Be her safe space, her sounding board, her biggest cheerleader. Encourage her to talk about her fears and hopes for the future. Help her find healthy ways to manage stress, whether it's through prenatal yoga, meditation, or simply spending time in nature.

And don't forget to share in the joy! Celebrate milestones like hearing the baby's heartbeat for the first time or feeling those first kicks. Take photos, write letters to your unborn child, and create memories that will last a lifetime.

Your journey through fatherhood begins now, not in the delivery room. By supporting your partner through the physical and emotional challenges of pregnancy, you're not only strengthening your bond as a couple, but also laying the groundwork for a healthy and happy family.

Building a Strong Foundation: Communication and Teamwork During Pregnancy.

The foundation of any successful relationship, be it a marriage, a friendship, or a business partnership, is built on trust, communication, and teamwork. In the context of impending parenthood, these pillars become even more crucial. The journey through pregnancy and beyond is a marathon, not a sprint, and it requires a united front to navigate the inevitable challenges and celebrate the triumphs.

Think of yourselves as co-pilots on a transatlantic flight. Each of you has a specific role to play, but you're both working towards the same destination: a safe and joyful landing with your precious cargo. The pilot, in this case, is the expectant mother, her body undergoing remarkable changes as it nurtures and grows a new life. As the co-pilot, your role is to provide unwavering support, clear communication, and a steady hand on the controls.

Communication is the fuel that powers your partnership. It's the exchange of information, thoughts, feelings, and expectations that keeps your relationship on track. During pregnancy, open and honest communication becomes even more essential as you navigate the uncharted territory of impending parenthood.

I vividly remember the early days of my wife's pregnancy. We were both excited but also overwhelmed by the sheer magnitude of what lay ahead. We had endless questions, concerns, and dreams for our future family. We quickly realized that the only way to navigate this new terrain was to talk openly and honestly with each other.

We established a ritual of nightly check-ins, where we would discuss everything from our fears and anxieties to our hopes and aspirations for our child. We shared articles and books we had read, discussed our birth plan, and debated baby names. Some nights were filled with laughter and excitement, while others were marked by tears and frustration. But through it all, we learned to listen to each other, to validate each other's feelings, and to compromise when necessary.

This open dialogue not only strengthened our bond as a couple, but also helped us prepare for the challenges of parenthood. By the time our daughter was born, we had already established a solid foundation of trust and communication that would serve us well in the years to come.

Teamwork is another essential ingredient in building a strong foundation during pregnancy. It's about recognizing that you're both in this together, working towards a common goal. It's about sharing responsibilities, supporting each other's strengths, and compensating for each other's weaknesses.

This might mean taking on more household chores while your partner is dealing with morning sickness or fatigue. It might involve attending prenatal appointments together, researching baby products, or preparing the nursery. It might also mean simply being there for each other, offering a listening ear or a shoulder to cry on.

Remember, pregnancy is a time of immense physical and emotional strain for your partner. By stepping up and sharing the load, you're not only easing her burden, but also showing her that you're committed to this journey together.

Teamwork also involves making shared decisions about your future as a family. This might include discussing your parenting philosophies, financial plans, and childcare arrangements. It's important to be open and honest about your expectations and to find common ground where you can. Remember, there's no one-size-fits-all approach to parenting, and the best way to find what works for your family is through collaboration and compromise.

As you build your foundation of communication and teamwork, it's important to be mindful of potential roadblocks. One common challenge is the issue of control. As the pregnancy progresses, your partner may feel like she's losing control of her body and her life. She might become more sensitive to your suggestions or feel like you're not taking her concerns seriously.

It's important to be patient and understanding during these times. Reassure your partner that you're there to support her, not control her. Listen to her concerns, validate her feelings, and offer your help without judgment. Remember, this is her journey too, and she needs to feel empowered and respected throughout the process.

Another potential challenge is the issue of differing expectations. You and your partner may have different ideas about what parenthood will look like, how you'll divide responsibilities, or what kind of parenting style you'll adopt. These differences can lead to misunderstandings, disagreements, and even resentment.

The key to overcoming these challenges is to maintain open lines of communication and to be willing to compromise. Talk about your expectations, fears, and hopes for the future. Be flexible and open to adjusting your plans as needed. Remember, parenthood is a constantly evolving journey, and your expectations may need to shift along the way.

Building a strong foundation during pregnancy is an investment in your future as a family. By prioritizing communication, teamwork, and mutual respect, you're creating a solid base upon which to build a loving, supportive, and joyful home for your child. It's a journey filled with challenges, but also with incredible rewards. So, embrace the adventure together, hand in hand, and step confidently into the next chapter of your lives.

Chapter 3

The First Trimester: Navigating the Early Days

"A grand adventure is about to begin." - Winnie the Pooh

As the initial wave of emotions settles and the reality of impending fatherhood sinks in, you and your partner embark on an incredible journey together – the first trimester of pregnancy. It's a time of rapid change and development, both for the tiny life growing inside your partner's womb and for your evolving roles as expectant parents. The first 12 weeks are a whirlwind of emotions, physical changes, and a steep learning curve as you both adjust to this new chapter in your lives.

In the first few weeks, your partner's body begins its miraculous transformation. Although she may not be showing yet, a tiny cluster of cells is rapidly dividing and growing inside her uterus. By week four, this cluster has developed into an embryo, a minuscule being with a beating heart. By week eight, the embryo has transformed into a fetus, and its major organs have begun to form. By the end of the first trimester, your baby is about the size of a lime, with tiny fingers and toes, and can even make small movements.

As your baby grows, your partner's body undergoes a series of changes to accommodate and nourish this new life. Her hormone levels fluctuate, causing a variety of symptoms such as morning sickness, fatigue, and mood swings. Her breasts may become tender and swollen, and she might experience changes in her appetite and sense of smell.

While these changes are a natural part of pregnancy, they can be challenging and uncomfortable for your partner. As her supportive co-pilot, your role is to understand and empathize with her experiences, offering both practical and emotional support. This might mean preparing healthy meals, offering gentle massages, or simply listening with a compassionate ear.

Prenatal care is another crucial aspect of the first trimester. Regular checkups with a healthcare provider are essential for monitoring both the mother's and baby's health. These visits typically include blood tests, ultrasounds, and discussions about nutrition, exercise, and lifestyle modifications.

As the expectant father, your involvement in prenatal care is invaluable. Attend appointments with your partner, ask questions, and take notes. Your presence not only provides emotional support but also demonstrates your commitment to your growing family. You can also help your partner track her appointments, medications, and any concerns she may have.

I remember feeling a bit overwhelmed during our first prenatal visit. The doctor rattled off a list of tests and precautions, and I struggled to keep up. But I made a conscious effort to be present and engaged, asking questions and taking notes. I realized that being informed and involved was not only beneficial for my partner, but also for my own peace of mind.

In addition to doctor's visits, a healthy lifestyle is crucial during pregnancy. Eating a balanced diet rich in fruits, vegetables, and whole grains can provide essential nutrients for both mother and baby. Regular exercise, such as walking or prenatal yoga, can help maintain fitness, reduce stress, and improve sleep.

As a supportive partner, you can play a vital role in encouraging and facilitating a healthy lifestyle during pregnancy. This might mean cooking nutritious meals together, going for walks, or finding prenatal exercise classes you can attend together. You can also help your partner research safe and effective exercise options and create a comfortable and supportive environment for her to maintain an active lifestyle.

The first trimester can be a time of both excitement and anxiety. It's common for expectant mothers to experience a range of concerns and discomforts, from morning sickness and fatigue to mood swings and sleep disturbances. As her partner, your understanding and support can make a world of difference.

When I first learned my wife was pregnant, I was overjoyed. However, as the weeks progressed, I noticed a shift in her mood. She became more irritable, easily overwhelmed, and prone to tears. At first, I was confused and hurt. But after doing some research and talking to other dads, I realized that these mood swings were a normal part of pregnancy.

Armed with this knowledge, I was able to approach my wife's emotions with empathy and understanding. Instead of taking her mood swings personally, I offered a listening ear, a warm hug, or a funny movie to distract her. I made a conscious effort to be patient, kind, and supportive, even when her emotions were unpredictable.

In addition to emotional support, there are practical steps you can take to help alleviate your partner's discomforts. If she's struggling with morning sickness, offer to prepare bland meals, encourage her to eat small, frequent snacks, and make sure she stays hydrated. If she's experiencing fatigue, create a relaxing bedtime routine, encourage naps, and take on additional household chores to give her more time to rest.

The first trimester is just the beginning of an incredible journey. It's a time of transformation, growth, and endless possibilities. By understanding and supporting your partner through the physical and emotional changes of early pregnancy, you're not only strengthening your bond as a couple but also laying the foundation for a healthy and happy family.

What to Expect: Week-by-Week Development of Your Baby.

The first trimester of pregnancy is a time of astonishing transformation. Within the cozy haven of your partner's womb, a symphony of creation unfolds, each week revealing a new movement in the breathtaking masterpiece that is your baby. As an expectant father, understanding this week-by-week development isn't just about knowledge; it's about forging a deeper connection with your child, an emotional bond that begins long before their first breath.

In the initial weeks, the changes are invisible to the naked eye, but no less miraculous. A tiny cluster of cells, a mere speck in the grand scheme of things, is rapidly dividing and multiplying, laying the groundwork for the complex being that will soon emerge. By week four, this cluster has evolved into an embryo, a minuscule marvel with a pulsating heart—the first tangible sign of life, a rhythmic drumbeat echoing the promise of parenthood.

As the days turn into weeks, the embryo undergoes a metamorphosis, growing exponentially and taking on a more recognizable form. By week six, it's the size of a sweet pea, its tiny limbs budding, and its major organs—the brain, heart, lungs, and kidneys—beginning to take shape. It's a time of intense activity, a symphony of cellular differentiation and organogenesis, all orchestrated by a complex interplay of genetic instructions and environmental cues.

Week eight marks a significant milestone: the embryo officially becomes a fetus, a term that signifies the beginning of a recognizably human form. Though still no bigger than a kidney bean, the fetus now boasts tiny arms and legs, budding fingers and toes, and a tail that will soon disappear. Its heart, a four-chambered marvel, beats with a steady rhythm, pumping oxygen-rich blood throughout its rapidly developing body.

By week ten, the fetus is roughly the size of a prune, its organs maturing and its senses awakening. Its tiny brain, a universe of neurons firing and connecting, is rapidly growing, laying the foundation for a lifetime of learning and discovery. Though you can't feel it yet, your baby is already moving, stretching its limbs, and exploring its watery world.

The end of the first trimester, week twelve, reveals a fetus that is now about the size of a lime. Its major organs are fully formed, its facial features are becoming more distinct, and its fingernails and toenails are starting to emerge. It can now swallow, kick, hiccup, and even suck its thumb, a testament to the remarkable complexity and resilience of human life.

I still recall the awe and wonder I felt when I first saw my child on the ultrasound screen. It was like peering into a secret world, a hidden universe where life was unfolding in real-time. The sight of that tiny, pulsating heart filled me with a profound sense of love and responsibility.

As the weeks progressed, each ultrasound became a cherished ritual, a window into the miraculous transformation taking place within my wife's body. We watched in amazement as our baby grew and developed, marveling at its tiny fingers and toes, its delicate features, and its increasingly coordinated movements.

The first trimester is a time of both wonder and apprehension. It's normal to have questions and concerns, to worry about your partner's health and your baby's well-being. But it's also a time to celebrate the miracle of life and embrace the profound joy of impending parenthood.

This is just the beginning of your journey as a father. By staying informed, engaged, and supportive, you can play an active role in your baby's development and lay the foundation for a lifetime of love and connection.

Prenatal Care Essentials: Doctor's Visits, Nutrition, and Exercise.

As the reality of impending fatherhood sets in and you marvel at the miraculous transformation occurring within your partner's body, it's time to shift gears and focus on the practical aspects of ensuring a healthy pregnancy. Prenatal care is the cornerstone of this journey, a series of essential check-ups, screenings, and lifestyle adjustments designed to safeguard both the mother's and baby's well-being. It's a collaborative effort, a partnership between the expectant parents and their healthcare provider, aimed at nurturing a thriving pregnancy and preparing for a smooth delivery.

Think of prenatal care as a roadmap, guiding you through the various stages of pregnancy and providing crucial information at each milestone. It's a proactive approach to healthcare, designed to identify and address any potential issues early on, ensuring the best possible outcomes for both mother and child.

The cornerstone of prenatal care is regular doctor's visits. These appointments typically begin in the first trimester and continue throughout the pregnancy, with increasing frequency as the due date approaches. During these visits, your partner's healthcare provider will conduct various tests and screenings to monitor her health and the baby's development.

These tests may include blood pressure checks, urine tests, weight measurements, and ultrasounds. Blood tests can detect potential issues such as anemia, gestational diabetes, and infections. Urine tests can assess kidney function and screen for urinary tract infections. Weight measurements help track the mother's overall health and ensure that she's gaining weight at a healthy rate. Ultrasounds provide a visual representation of the baby's development, allowing the healthcare provider to assess its growth, anatomy, and overall well-being.

As an expectant father, your presence at these appointments is invaluable. It shows your partner that you're invested in her well-being and the health of your growing family. It also gives you the opportunity to ask questions, learn about the various tests and procedures, and become an active participant in your partner's prenatal care.

I remember feeling a mix of excitement and anxiety during our first prenatal visit. The doctor's office was filled with expectant mothers, each with their own unique story and set of concerns. As we waited for our turn, I couldn't help but feel a sense of awe and wonder at the miracle of life unfolding within my wife's body.

When we finally met with the doctor, I was impressed by her warmth and attentiveness. She patiently answered all _our questions, explaining the various tests and procedures in detail. She also emphasized the importance of maintaining a healthy lifestyle during pregnancy, stressing the significance of nutrition and exercise._

Nutrition plays a crucial role in supporting a healthy pregnancy. A well-balanced diet rich in fruits, vegetables, whole grains, lean protein, and healthy fats provides essential nutrients for both mother and baby. These nutrients are essential for fetal growth and development, as well as for maintaining the mother's energy levels and overall well-being.

It's important for expectant mothers to avoid certain foods during pregnancy, such as raw or undercooked meat, fish high in mercury, unpasteurized dairy products, and excessive caffeine. They should also limit their intake of processed foods, sugary drinks, and unhealthy fats.

As a supportive partner, you can play an active role in promoting healthy eating habits during pregnancy. This might involve cooking nutritious meals together, stocking the fridge with healthy snacks, and researching recipes that cater to your partner's changing tastes and preferences.

Exercise is another vital component of prenatal care. Regular physical activity can help improve circulation, reduce back pain and fatigue, and prepare the body for labor and delivery. It can also help boost mood, reduce stress, and promote better sleep.

Expectant mothers should aim for at least 30 minutes of moderate-intensity exercise most days of the week. This could include activities like walking, swimming, prenatal yoga, or low-impact aerobics. It's important to listen to your body and avoid overexertion.

As a supportive partner, you can encourage and facilitate your partner's exercise routine. This might involve joining her for walks, finding prenatal exercise classes you can attend together, or simply creating a supportive and encouraging environment for her to stay active.

Prenatal care is not just about medical checkups and healthy habits; it's also about emotional well-being. Pregnancy can be a time of heightened emotions, and it's important for expectant mothers to have a safe and supportive space to express their feelings.

As a partner, you can provide this emotional support by listening attentively, validating her emotions, and offering words of encouragement. You can also help her find healthy ways to manage stress, such as relaxation techniques, meditation, or spending time in nature.

Remember, pregnancy is a journey, not a destination. By embracing prenatal care as a collaborative effort, you can ensure a healthy and fulfilling experience for both you and your partner. With knowledge, support, and a commitment to a healthy lifestyle, you can lay the foundation for a thriving pregnancy and a smooth transition into parenthood.

Chapter 4

The Second Trimester: Growing Together

"We made a wish, and you came true." –
Anonymous

My friend, Mark, always had a knack for finding humor in the most unexpected situations. When his wife entered her second trimester of pregnancy, their once quiet evenings transformed into a symphony of bizarre cravings and unexpected emotions. One night, after a particularly intense craving for pickles and peanut butter, Mark found himself standing in the middle of the night at a 24-hour supermarket, clutching a jar of each in his hands. He turned to the cashier, a bemused look on his face, and quipped, *"Guess someone's got a bun in the oven, and it ain't me!"*

The second trimester often marks a turning point in the pregnancy journey, a time when the initial shock and awe give way to a deeper sense of connection and anticipation. For the expectant mother, it's a time of blossoming, both physically and emotionally. The morning sickness often subsides, energy levels rebound, and a newfound radiance illuminates her face. The baby bump, once a subtle curve, now proudly announces its presence, a tangible reminder of the miracle unfolding within.

But it's not just the physical changes that are noteworthy. The second trimester is also a period of significant emotional growth for both parents. As the baby's movements become more pronounced, the bond between mother and child deepens. The fluttering kicks and gentle nudges serve as a constant reminder of the precious life growing within, fostering a sense of love and protectiveness that's hard to describe.

For the expectant father, the second trimester offers a unique opportunity to connect with the baby in the womb. It's a time to establish a bond that will last a lifetime, a foundation of love and support that will shape the child's future. While the mother experiences the physical sensations of pregnancy firsthand, the father can play an active role in fostering this connection through various means.

One of the most powerful ways for dads to bond with their unborn child is through touch. Placing a hand on the mother's belly and feeling the baby's movements is an intimate and awe-inspiring experience. It's a tangible reminder of the life growing within and a way to physically connect with the child before they even enter the world.

The first time I felt my daughter kick. It was a surreal moment, a sudden jolt of movement that took my breath away. I placed my hand on my wife's belly, and as I felt the rhythmic kicks and jabs, a wave of emotion washed over me. It was a feeling of pure joy, of wonder, of a love that transcended words.

In addition to touch, sound is another powerful tool for bonding with your baby in the womb. Talking, singing, or reading to your unborn child can stimulate their developing senses and create a sense of familiarity and comfort. Some studies even suggest that babies can recognize their parents' voices before they're born.

I made it a habit to read to my daughter every night before bed. I would sit beside my wife, gently stroking her belly, and read aloud from children's books, poetry, or even the newspaper. It didn't matter what I read, as long as I was sharing my voice and my love with my unborn child.

As the second trimester progresses, it's also important to start thinking about the practical preparations for parenthood. This includes attending birthing classes, creating a birth plan, setting up the nursery, and making financial arrangements for the baby's arrival.

Birthing classes provide valuable information about labor and delivery, pain management techniques, and newborn care. They also offer a supportive environment for expectant parents to connect with each other and share their hopes and concerns.

Creating a birth plan is a way to communicate your preferences for labor and delivery with your healthcare provider. It can include details about pain management, who you want present during the birth, and what kind of environment you envision for welcoming your child into the world.

Setting up the nursery is a fun and exciting way to prepare for your baby's arrival. It's a chance to create a safe and nurturing space for your child, filled with love, warmth, and all the essentials they'll need.

Financial planning is another crucial aspect of preparing for parenthood. Babies can be expensive, and it's important to have a clear understanding of your financial situation and make necessary adjustments to accommodate your growing family.

The second trimester is a time of growth, both for the baby and for the parents-to-be. It's a time to connect, to prepare, and to embrace the anticipation of what's to come. By actively participating in this journey, you can forge a strong bond with your child and create a loving and supportive environment for your growing family.

Feeling the Kicks: Bonding with Your Baby in the Womb.

There's a unique kind of magic that fills the air when you first feel your baby's movements within your partner's womb. It's a sensation unlike any other, a flutter, a kick, a gentle roll that serves as a tangible reminder of the precious life growing inside. This magical moment is often referred to as "quickening," and it typically occurs around the 16th to 25th week of pregnancy. For many fathers, it's a profound experience, a visceral connection to their unborn child that solidifies the reality of impending parenthood.

I'll never forget the first time I felt my daughter kick. It was a quiet evening at home, my wife and I nestled on the couch, her belly gently rounded beneath her favorite maternity dress. I had placed my hand on her stomach, as I often did, hoping to catch a glimpse of movement. Suddenly, I felt a distinct thump, a gentle nudge against my palm. It was as if a tiny butterfly had taken flight within my wife's womb.

I looked at her with wide eyes, a mixture of surprise and elation washing over me. "Did you feel that?" I asked, my voice barely above a whisper. She smiled, her eyes sparkling with joy, and nodded. "Yes," she whispered back, "that was her."

In that moment, time seemed to stand still. A wave of emotions swept over me: awe, wonder, love, and a profound sense of responsibility. I realized that I was no longer just a husband, a friend, or a professional. I was a father, connected to my child in a way that transcended words.

Feeling your baby's kicks is a transformative experience, a rite of passage into fatherhood. It's a reminder that you're not just a bystander in this journey; you're an active participant, a co-creator of life. And as you continue to feel those gentle movements, your bond with your unborn child will only deepen.

But bonding with your baby in the womb goes beyond simply feeling their kicks. It's a multifaceted experience that involves engaging all your senses and tapping into your innate paternal instincts.

One of the simplest and most effective ways to connect with your baby is through touch. Place your hands on your partner's belly and feel for movements. As the baby grows, you'll be able to distinguish between kicks, punches, and even hiccups. You can also try gently massaging your partner's belly, which can help soothe the baby and promote relaxation.

Talking to your baby is another powerful way to bond. Share your thoughts, feelings, and hopes for the future. Read aloud from your favorite books, sing lullabies, or simply tell your baby how much you love them. Your voice will become a familiar and comforting presence in their world, even before they enter it.

Music is another wonderful way to connect with your unborn child. Play soothing melodies or upbeat tunes, and observe how your baby responds. Some babies become more active when they hear music, while others seem to relax and calm down.

Experiment with different genres and artists to discover what your baby enjoys.

As your baby's senses develop, they become increasingly aware of their environment. They can hear your voice, feel your touch, and even sense changes in your partner's mood. By engaging with your baby in the womb, you're not only fostering a bond, but also contributing to their development.

Studies have shown that babies who are exposed to language and music in the womb tend to have better language and cognitive skills later in life. They are also more likely to be calm and content, and to have a stronger attachment to their parents.

Bonding with your baby in the womb is not just about the baby; it's also about strengthening your relationship with your partner. Sharing this experience with your partner can bring you closer together, deepening your love and appreciation for each other.

I remember the nights when my wife and I would lie in bed, our hands intertwined on her belly, feeling our daughter's gentle movements. We would talk to her, sing to her, and marvel at the miracle growing inside. These intimate moments created a sense of unity and purpose, a shared experience that strengthened our bond and prepared us for the joys and challenges of parenthood.

As you continue on this journey, don't be afraid to experiment and find what works best for you and your family. Some fathers prefer to write letters to their unborn child, while others create playlists of their favorite songs. Some dads even talk to their baby while they're at work, sending their love and encouragement across the miles.

The most important thing is to be present, engaged, and open to the experience. Embrace the wonder of life growing within your partner, and cherish the precious moments you share with your unborn child.

These early connections will lay the foundation for a lifetime of love, laughter, and shared adventure.

Preparing for Parenthood: Birthing Classes, Nursery Planning, and Financial Considerations.

As the thrill of feeling your baby's first kicks settles into a comforting rhythm, the second trimester becomes a pivotal time for preparing for the practical realities of parenthood. It's a shift from the awe-inspiring wonder of creation to the tangible steps you can take to welcome your little one into a loving and nurturing environment. Remember those late-night supermarket runs for pickles and peanut butter? Now, it's time to channel that energy into more structured preparations that will ease your transition into parenthood.

First on the list is birthing classes. While the thought of attending a class might seem daunting or even unnecessary, trust me, it's a game-changer. These classes aren't just about breathing exercises and pain management techniques (although those are certainly important!). They're about empowering you and your partner with knowledge and confidence.

Think of birthing classes as a crash course in labor and delivery. You'll learn about the different stages of labor, the various pain relief options available, and what to expect during those first few hours after your baby is born. You'll also have the opportunity to ask questions, share your concerns, and connect with other expectant parents who are going through the same experience.

My wife and I attended a birthing class led by a veteran midwife, and it was one of the best decisions we made during our pregnancy. We learned so much about the birthing process, and it helped us feel more prepared and less anxious about the big day. We also made some wonderful friends in the class, couples who were going through the same journey as us. It was comforting to know that we weren't alone in our excitement and nervousness.

Along with birthing classes, creating a birth plan is another crucial step in preparing for your baby's arrival. It's a document that outlines your preferences for labor and delivery, such as your desired pain management options, who you want to be present during the birth, and any specific requests you have for the hospital staff.

While it's important to have a birth plan, it's equally important to be flexible. Remember, childbirth is unpredictable, and things don't always go according to plan. The key is to be open to different scenarios and trust your healthcare provider's expertise.

As you prepare for your baby's arrival, it's also time to start thinking about the nursery. This is where your little one will spend their first few months, so you want to create a space that's safe, comfortable, and nurturing. It doesn't have to be elaborate or expensive; even a simple, well-organized space can be a haven for your newborn.

Start by choosing a room that's well-ventilated and gets plenty of natural light. Paint the walls a calming color, like soft pastels or neutrals. Invest in a comfortable crib or bassinet, a changing table, and a rocking chair or glider. You'll also need diapers, wipes, onesies, and other baby essentials.

Don't forget to personalize the space with meaningful touches, such as framed photos, artwork, or a mobile. This is your chance to create a space that reflects your love and excitement for your growing family.

While decorating the nursery can be a fun and creative project, it's important to keep safety in mind. Make sure the crib meets safety standards, and avoid using any furniture or decorations that could pose a hazard to your baby.

Financial planning is another crucial aspect of preparing for parenthood. Babies can be expensive, and it's important to have a clear understanding of your financial situation and make necessary adjustments to accommodate your growing family.

Start by creating a budget that includes all the expenses associated with having a baby, such as diapers, formula, clothes, childcare, and medical bills. Consider any changes you might need to make to your lifestyle or spending habits.

It's also a good idea to start saving for your child's future. Consider opening a college savings account or investing in a life insurance policy. By planning ahead, you can ensure that your child has the resources they need to thrive.

Preparing for parenthood is a journey, not a destination. It's about taking small steps each day, learning as you go, and embracing the excitement and challenges that come with this new chapter in your life. By attending birthing classes, creating a birth plan, setting up the nursery, and planning financially, you're laying the groundwork for a smooth and joyful transition into parenthood.

Chapter 5

The Third Trimester: The Final Countdown

"The best time to plant a tree was 20 years ago. The second best time is now." – Chinese Proverb

As the final act of your partner's pregnancy unfolds, a sense of anticipation fills the air. The third trimester, often referred to as the home stretch, is a whirlwind of preparations, emotions, and a touch of nervous excitement. It's a time when the abstract concept of "baby" transforms into a tangible reality, a little human being who will soon grace your lives with their presence. And as the due date draws near, it's time to roll up your sleeves and get your home ready for this momentous arrival.

Nesting, the instinctive urge to prepare a safe and comfortable haven for your newborn, kicks into high gear during the third trimester. It's a primal instinct, a biological imperative that compels expectant parents to create a nurturing environment for their little one. Embrace this instinct, for it's a beautiful and practical way to channel your energy and excitement into tangible actions.

Start by decluttering and organizing your living space. Clear out any unnecessary items, create designated areas for baby gear, and ensure that everything is easily accessible. This will not only make your home more functional but also create a sense of calm and order amidst the whirlwind of new parenthood.

Next, focus on creating a safe and comfortable sleep space for your baby. Invest in a sturdy crib or bassinet that meets safety standards, and choose a firm mattress and fitted sheets. Avoid using soft bedding, pillows, or bumpers, as these can pose a suffocation risk.

In addition to the crib, you'll need a changing table stocked with diapers, wipes, and other essentials. A comfortable rocking chair or glider can be a lifesaver for late-night feedings and soothing sessions. And don't forget to create a cozy corner for yourself, where you can relax and bond with your baby.

As you prepare your home, it's also important to stock up on essential baby gear. This includes a car seat, stroller, baby carrier, bottles, formula (if you're not breastfeeding), diapers, wipes, onesies, sleepers, and burp cloths. It's also a good idea to have a few pacifiers, teething toys, and a baby monitor on hand.

While shopping for baby gear can be a fun and exciting experience, it's important to prioritize safety and functionality over aesthetics. Do your research, read reviews, and choose products that meet safety standards and are appropriate for your baby's age and development.

As the due date approaches, it's also essential to pack a hospital bag for both mom and dad. This bag should include everything you'll need for labor, delivery, and the first few days postpartum.

For mom, pack comfortable clothes to wear during labor and after delivery, nursing bras and pads, toiletries, snacks, a phone charger, and any comfort items she might want, such as a favorite pillow or blanket. For dad, pack a change of clothes, toiletries, snacks, a book or magazine, and a camera to capture those precious first moments.

The third trimester can also be a time of heightened anxiety and stress. As the reality of labor and delivery looms closer, it's natural to feel a mix of excitement and apprehension. The key is to acknowledge these feelings and find healthy ways to manage them.

I could remember feeling a surge of anxiety as my wife's due date approached. I worried about her safety during labor, about my ability to support her, and about the unknown challenges of parenthood. To manage my stress, I started practicing mindfulness techniques, such as meditation and deep breathing exercises. I also made a conscious effort to spend quality time with my wife, talking about our fears and hopes for the future.

If you're feeling overwhelmed, don't hesitate to talk to your partner, a trusted friend or family member, or a therapist. It's also important to prioritize self-care during this time. Get enough sleep, eat healthy foods, exercise regularly, and take time for activities you enjoy.

Preparing for labor and delivery can also help alleviate anxiety. Attend birthing classes, review your birth plan with your healthcare provider, and pack your hospital bag well in advance. Knowing that you're prepared can give you a sense of control and confidence as you approach the big day.

The third trimester is a time of anticipation, excitement, and a touch of nervousness. It's a time to prepare your home, pack your hospital bag, and manage any anxieties that may arise. By focusing on the practical aspects of preparation and prioritizing your well-being, you can approach this final stage of pregnancy with confidence and anticipation. Remember, you're not alone on this journey. Millions of fathers before you have walked this path, and millions more will follow in your footsteps.

As the third trimester progresses and the reality of your baby's arrival becomes more tangible, a primal instinct known as "nesting" often kicks in. It's a surge of energy and motivation, a biological imperative that compels expectant parents to prepare their home for the newest member of the family. For many, it's a flurry of cleaning, organizing, and decorating, a whirlwind of activity fueled by anticipation and a desire to create a safe and nurturing haven for their little one. Remember Mark, my friend who braved the late-night supermarket run for pickles and peanut butter? Well, as his wife's due date approached, his nesting instincts went into overdrive.

One weekend, I found him perched on a ladder, meticulously painting the nursery walls a soothing shade of lavender. He had meticulously researched the perfect color, one that was said to promote calmness and serenity in infants. His usually cluttered toolbox was now neatly organized, each tool in its designated spot. He even insisted on hand-washing all the baby clothes, meticulously inspecting each garment for loose threads or imperfections.

Mark's nesting frenzy might seem excessive to some, but it's a testament to the deep-seated desire to create a safe and welcoming environment for a new baby. Nesting is not just about aesthetics; it's about preparing a functional and nurturing space where your little one can thrive.

Start by decluttering and organizing your living spaces. This might involve purging closets, donating unused items, and creating designated areas for baby gear. A well-organized home not only makes it easier to navigate with a newborn in tow but also promotes a sense of calm and tranquility, which can be invaluable during the often chaotic early days of parenthood.

Next, focus on the nursery. This is where your baby will spend most of their time in the first few months, so it's important to create a space that's both safe and stimulating. Choose a room that's well-ventilated and receives plenty of natural light. If possible, opt for a room that's close to your bedroom, making it easier to respond to your baby's needs during the night.

When it comes to decorating, keep it simple and functional. Choose a calming color palette, such as soft pastels or neutrals, and avoid overly stimulating patterns or designs. Invest in a sturdy crib or bassinet that meets safety standards, and choose a firm mattress and fitted sheets. Skip the fluffy blankets, pillows, and bumpers, as these can pose a suffocation risk for newborns.

Consider adding a comfortable rocking chair or glider to the nursery. This will be your sanctuary for late-night feedings, soothing sessions, and quiet moments of bonding with your baby. A changing table stocked with diapers, wipes, and other essentials will also come in handy.

As you prepare the nursery, don't forget about the rest of your home. Baby-proof your living spaces by securing cabinets and drawers, covering electrical outlets, and installing safety gates. Remove any potential hazards, such as loose cords, small objects, or toxic plants.

In addition to preparing your home, it's also important to stock up on essential baby gear. This includes a car seat, stroller, baby carrier, bottles, formula (if you're not breastfeeding), diapers, wipes, onesies, sleepers, and burp cloths. You might also want to consider purchasing a baby monitor, a white noise machine, and a few comforting toys and books.

You don't need to buy everything at once. Start with the essentials, and then gradually add items as you need them. You can also ask friends and family for hand-me-downs or borrow items from them.

Nesting is a personal journey, and what works for one family may not work for another. The most important thing is to create a space that feels safe, welcoming, and nurturing for your little one. As you embark on this exciting project, remember that you're not just preparing your home for a baby; you're building a foundation for a lifetime of love, laughter, and memories.

Packing Your Hospital Bag: Essentials for Labor and Delivery.

The nesting instinct isn't limited to just preparing your home. As the countdown to D-Day (delivery day!) intensifies, a crucial task looms large: packing your hospital bag. This isn't just any old overnight bag; it's a carefully curated collection of essentials designed to make your hospital stay as comfortable and stress-free as possible. It's your survival kit for the whirlwind of labor, delivery, and those precious first moments with your newborn.

Picture this: You're awakened in the dead of night by your partner's contractions. Adrenaline surges through your veins as you scramble to gather your belongings and rush to the hospital. In the midst of this chaos, the last thing you want to worry about is whether you've packed everything you need.

That's where the hospital bag comes in. It's your insurance policy against forgotten essentials, a lifeline that ensures you have everything you need to support your partner and welcome your baby into the world. But what exactly should you pack? Let's break it down into two categories: essentials for mom and essentials for dad.

For mom, comfort is key. Pack loose-fitting, comfortable clothing that she can wear during labor and after delivery. A soft robe and slippers can add an extra layer of coziness. Don't forget nursing bras and pads, as well as toiletries like shampoo, conditioner, soap, toothbrush, and toothpaste.

Pack a few snacks and drinks to keep her energy levels up during labor. Nuts, dried fruit, granola bars, and juice boxes are all good options. And don't forget a phone charger so she can stay connected with loved ones and document those precious first moments.

For dad, the hospital bag should be a mix of practical and comfort items. Pack a change of clothes, including comfortable pants, a t-shirt, and a sweater or jacket in case the hospital is chilly. Bring toiletries, snacks, and a water bottle to keep yourself hydrated and energized.

Consider packing a book, magazine, or tablet to keep yourself occupied during downtime. You might also want to bring a camera or smartphone to capture those first precious photos of your newborn.

Now, let's talk about those common anxieties that tend to crop up during the third trimester. The anticipation of labor and delivery can be a source of stress for both expectant parents. Will the labor be long and difficult? Will there be complications? Will I be a good birth partner?

These are all valid concerns, and it's perfectly normal to feel anxious or overwhelmed at times. The key is to acknowledge these feelings and find healthy ways to manage them. Talk to your partner about your fears, and listen to hers. Share your hopes and expectations for the birth, and create a birth plan that reflects your shared values and preferences.

Remember that knowledge is power. Educate yourself about the stages of labor, pain management options, and what to expect during the postpartum period. Attend birthing classes, read books and articles, and talk to other parents who have been through it.

Another way to manage stress is to practice relaxation techniques, such as deep breathing, meditation, or prenatal yoga. These techniques can help you stay calm and centered during labor and delivery, and can also be helpful for managing anxiety and promoting sleep during pregnancy.

Don't underestimate the power of physical touch. Offer your partner massages, foot rubs, and back rubs to help ease discomfort and promote relaxation. A warm bath or shower can also be soothing.

Remember, you're not alone in this journey. Millions of fathers have walked this path before you, and millions more will follow. By leaning on your support system, educating yourself, and prioritizing self-care, you can approach the final countdown with confidence and excitement.

As for me, I vividly recall the night my wife went into labor. We had packed our hospital bags weeks in advance, and we were as prepared as we could be. But as the contractions intensified, my nerves started to fray. I found myself pacing the hospital room, clutching my wife's hand, and offering words of encouragement. When our daughter finally arrived, all the anxiety melted away, replaced by an overwhelming sense of love and awe.

In that moment, I realized that all the preparation in the world couldn't fully prepare me for the intensity and beauty of childbirth. But it did give me the confidence and knowledge to support my wife and welcome my daughter into the world with open arms. And that, my friend, is the true essence of fatherhood.

Chapter 6

Labor and Delivery: Your Role as a Birth Partner

"Labor is hard work, but it's the most rewarding work you'll ever do." - Anonymous

As your partner's due date approaches, the anticipation and excitement reach a fever pitch. The culmination of months of preparation, the labor and delivery experience is a pivotal moment in your journey to parenthood. It's a time of intense emotions, physical demands, and a profound transformation as you welcome your new baby into the world. But what exactly should you expect during this momentous event? How can you best support your partner as she navigates the challenges of labor? And what role can you play in creating a positive and empowering birth experience?

Labor and delivery is not a one-size-fits-all experience. It varies from woman to woman, and even from one pregnancy to the next. However, there are distinct stages that most women go through, each with its own unique characteristics and challenges. Understanding these stages can help you anticipate what's to come and prepare for your role as a supportive birth partner.

The first stage of labor, known as the latent phase, is often the longest and can last for several hours or even days. During this phase, the cervix begins to soften, thin out, and dilate. Contractions are usually mild and irregular at first, gradually becoming stronger and more frequent as labor progresses. Your partner may experience backache, cramping, and a bloody show, which is a discharge of mucus from the cervix.

As a birth partner, your role during this phase is to provide comfort and reassurance. Encourage your partner to rest, hydrate, and eat light snacks. Help her find comfortable positions, offer back rubs or massages, and provide distraction through conversation or entertainment. Your presence and support can make a world of difference in helping her manage the early stages of labor.

The active phase of labor is when things start to get more intense. Contractions become stronger, longer, and more frequent, and your partner's cervix dilates further. This is the time when many women choose to utilize pain relief options, such as epidurals or nitrous oxide.

Your role during this phase is to be a constant source of support and encouragement. Help your partner breathe through contractions, offer ice chips or a cool cloth, and remind her of her strength and resilience. You can also help her change positions, as movement can often ease discomfort and promote labor progress.

The transition phase is the most challenging and intense part of labor. Contractions are at their peak intensity, and your partner's cervix dilates to its full capacity. She may feel overwhelmed, exhausted, and even discouraged.

This is the time when your support is most crucial. Remind her that she's doing an amazing job, that she's strong and capable, and that you're right there with her every step of the way. Offer words of encouragement, hold her hand, and provide a calming presence. Your unwavering support can help her navigate the final stretch of labor and prepare for the pushing stage.

The pushing stage is when your partner's body begins to push the baby down and out of the birth canal. This can be a physically demanding and emotionally intense experience. Your role is to continue offering encouragement and support, helping her find comfortable positions, and reminding her to breathe and push effectively.

The final stage of labor is the delivery of the placenta. This is usually a relatively quick and painless process, but it's still important for your partner to rest and recover after the exertion of childbirth.

Throughout the entire labor and delivery process, your emotional support is invaluable. Remember, childbirth is not just a physical event; it's a profound emotional experience. Your partner may feel vulnerable, scared, and overwhelmed. Your presence, your touch, and your words of encouragement can provide a sense of comfort and security, helping her feel safe and supported during this transformative time.

I recall vividly the moment my wife went into labor. The anticipation and excitement we had been feeling for months suddenly turned into a whirlwind of activity. As we

But as labor progressed, I quickly realized that childbirth rarely follows a script. My wife's contractions became more intense than we had anticipated, and she opted for an epidural for pain relief. I stayed by her side, holding her hand, offering words of encouragement, and reminding her of her strength.

As the hours passed, I witnessed firsthand the incredible power and resilience of the female body. I watched my wife transform into a warrior, her determination and focus unwavering. And when our daughter finally arrived, her tiny cries filling the room, I was overwhelmed with emotion. It was a moment of pure joy, of profound love, of a connection that transcended words.

In that moment, I realized that my role as a birth partner was not just about providing physical and emotional support. It was about witnessing and honoring the miracle of life, about celebrating the strength and courage of my partner, and about embracing the transformative power of fatherhood.

Understanding Labor Stages: Early Labor, Active Labor, and Transition.

Imagine labor as a symphony, a carefully orchestrated performance with distinct movements, each building upon the last, culminating in a grand finale—the birth of your child. As a supportive partner, understanding the different stages of labor is like reading the musical score, allowing you to anticipate the rhythm, tempo, and intensity of each movement, and to provide the appropriate support and encouragement at every turn.

The first movement, known as early labor, is a gentle overture, a gradual awakening of the body in preparation for the main event. It's a time of subtle shifts and sensations, a gradual crescendo of contractions that signal the onset of labor. Your partner might experience mild, irregular contractions, a dull ache in her lower back, or a feeling of pressure in her pelvis.

During this stage, it's important to create a calm and comfortable environment for your partner. Encourage her to rest, hydrate, and nourish her body with light snacks. Offer a comforting touch, a warm bath, or a gentle massage. Distract her with conversation, music, or a favorite movie. This is a time for patience and reassurance, for reminding her that you're in this together and that she's strong and capable.

As the symphony progresses, the second movement, active labor, takes center stage. The contractions become stronger, longer, and more frequent, propelling your partner into the heart of labor. Her cervix continues to dilate, and the baby descends further into the birth canal. This is typically the most challenging phase of labor, as the physical and emotional demands intensify.

Your role during active labor is to be a pillar of strength and support. Help your partner find comfortable positions, whether it's rocking on a birthing ball, leaning on you for support, or taking a warm shower. Offer words of encouragement, remind her of her breathing techniques, and celebrate each milestone as she progresses through labor.

This is also a time to advocate for your partner's needs. If she's experiencing intense pain, discuss pain management options with her healthcare provider. Whether it's an epidural, nitrous oxide, or other comfort measures, your role is to ensure that your partner feels informed and empowered to make decisions about her care.

As active labor reaches its crescendo, the third movement, transition, takes over. This is the shortest but most intense phase of labor, often described as a whirlwind of emotions and sensations. Contractions are at their peak intensity, coming in rapid succession, and your partner's cervix dilates to its full capacity.

During transition, your partner may feel overwhelmed, exhausted, and even discouraged. She might vocalize her pain or express doubts about her ability to continue. This is a critical moment, a turning point where your support can make all the difference.

Remind her that she's doing an amazing job, that she's strong and capable, and that the end is in sight. Offer unwavering encouragement, hold her hand, and provide a calming presence. Help her focus on her breathing, remind her of her goals, and celebrate each contraction as a step closer to meeting your baby.

In those moments, I realized that my role as a birth partner was not just about being a cheerleader or a coach. It was about being a witness to the raw power of creation, a silent observer of a woman's incredible journey into motherhood. It was about holding space for her pain, her fear, and her triumph.

As the final push approached, I felt a wave of anticipation wash over me. The end was near, and soon, we would meet our little one. I knew that the challenges of labor and delivery were just the beginning of our journey as parents, but in that moment, all that mattered was the love and connection that was about to blossom between us and our child.

Supporting Your Partner During Labor: Pain Management Techniques and Emotional Support.

Amidst the flurry of labor, my wife's grip tightened around my hand, her knuckles white with the intensity of each contraction. A shared glance, a silent understanding passed between us - this was it, the culmination of months of preparation, of dreams and anxieties intertwined. My mind raced back to the early days of her pregnancy, the first ultrasound where a tiny flicker on the screen confirmed our hopes and ignited a flame of anticipation in our hearts.

Now, in this dimly lit delivery room, that anticipation was about to be realized. But as the pain escalated, my focus shifted to providing the support my wife needed. I recalled the breathing exercises we'd practiced, the soothing words we'd exchanged during our birthing class. Now, it was time to put them into action.

With each contraction, I breathed with her, matching her rhythm, offering a steady counterpoint to the storm raging within her body. I massaged her back, whispered words of encouragement, and reminded her of her strength. I was her anchor, her lifeline, her unwavering source of support.

The room was a symphony of sensations – the rhythmic beeping of the heart monitor, the hushed voices of the medical staff, the raw, primal sounds of my wife's labor. It was a dance of pain and perseverance, of vulnerability and strength. And I was privileged to be her partner in this dance.

As the hours wore on, the contractions grew more intense, the breaks between them shorter. My wife's breathing grew ragged, her grip on my hand tighter. I could see the exhaustion etched on her face, but also the fierce determination that burned in her eyes.

Pain management became a priority. We had discussed our options beforehand, and she had opted for an epidural. As the anesthesiologist administered the medication, I held her close, whispering words of comfort and reassurance. The relief on her face was palpable, a testament to the power of modern medicine to ease the burden of childbirth.

But even with pain relief, labor is a marathon, not a sprint. As the hours turned into a sleepless night, I remained by her side, offering sips of water, wiping her brow, and adjusting her pillows. I watched in awe as she navigated the different stages of labor – the early contractions, the active labor, and the intense transition phase that marked the final stretch before delivery.

With each contraction, I felt a surge of adrenaline, a primal urge to protect and support my wife. I reminded her of the birthing affirmations we had practiced, of her strength and resilience, of the beautiful life we were about to welcome into the world.

And then, finally, the moment arrived. With a final push, our daughter emerged, her cries filling the room with a symphony of new life. As I cut the umbilical cord and held her in my arms for the first time, I was overcome with emotion. All the fear, anxiety, and anticipation melted away, replaced by an overwhelming sense of love and gratitude.

In that moment, I understood the true meaning of partnership in childbirth. It's about being present, both physically and emotionally. It's about offering unwavering support, even when things don't go according to plan. It's about celebrating the

strength and resilience of the woman you
love as she brings your child into the world.

Chapter 7

Welcoming Your Baby: The First Moments

"A new baby is like the beginning of all things- wonder, hope, a dream of possibilities." – Eda J. Le Shan

Did you know that within the first hour after birth, a newborn's sense of smell is so acute that they can recognize their mother's scent? This is just one of the many fascinating and miraculous aspects of the immediate postpartum period, a time of profound bonding, adjustment, and discovery for both parents and baby.

As the final push culminates in a cry that echoes the miracle of life, the delivery room transforms into a haven of raw emotion and unbridled joy. The air crackles with a palpable energy, a mix of relief, exhaustion, and overwhelming love. This is the *"golden*

118

hour," a precious window of time immediately after birth that's crucial for bonding and establishing a healthy start for your newborn.

In this sacred hour, skin-to-skin contact takes center stage. Placing your naked baby on your partner's bare chest fosters a deep connection, regulating the baby's body temperature, heart rate, and breathing. It also triggers the release of oxytocin, the "love hormone," in both mother and baby, strengthening their bond and promoting breastfeeding.

As a new dad, don't hesitate to participate in this intimate ritual. Hold your baby close, marvel at their tiny features, and whisper words of love and welcome. The warmth of your skin, the sound of your heartbeat, and the gentle rhythm of your breathing will soothe and comfort your newborn, creating a sense of security and trust.

Breastfeeding, if your partner chooses to do so, is another crucial aspect of the postpartum period. It's a natural and instinctive process, but it can also be challenging, especially in the early days. Your role as a supportive partner is to encourage and facilitate breastfeeding, offering practical assistance and emotional support.

Help your partner find comfortable positions for breastfeeding, ensure she's well-hydrated and nourished, and offer to burp or change the baby when needed. Be patient and understanding as she learns to navigate the nuances of breastfeeding, and celebrate her successes along the way. Remember, breastfeeding is a journey, and every drop of milk is a gift of love and nourishment for your baby.

While bonding and breastfeeding take center stage, the immediate postpartum period also involves various medical assessments for both mother and baby.

These assessments are designed to ensure their well-being and identify any potential issues early on.

For the mother, this might include checking her vital signs, assessing her bleeding, and monitoring her pain levels. The healthcare provider will also examine her perineum, the area between the vagina and anus, which may have been torn or cut during delivery.

For the baby, the initial assessments typically include measuring their weight and length, checking their reflexes, and assessing their overall health and development. The baby will also receive their first vaccinations and screenings for various conditions.

As a supportive partner, your role during these assessments is to be present, offer reassurance, and advocate for your partner's and baby's needs. Ask questions, clarify any concerns, and ensure that both mother and baby receive the best possible care.

The postpartum period is not without its challenges. Your partner's body is recovering from the physical demands of childbirth, and her hormones are fluctuating wildly. She may experience postpartum bleeding, perineal pain, and breast engorgement. Sleep deprivation and emotional vulnerability are also common.

As her partner, your support during this time is crucial. Help with household chores, prepare meals, and offer to take care of the baby so she can rest. Encourage her to talk about her feelings, and validate her emotions. Remind her that she's not alone and that you're there to support her through this transition.

Early bonding with your newborn is a precious gift, a foundation for a lifetime of love and connection. Take every opportunity to hold, cuddle, and talk to your baby. Skin-to-skin contact is especially important, as it promotes bonding, regulates the baby's body temperature, and reduces stress.

Engage in activities like reading, singing, and playing with your baby. Your voice, touch, and presence will soothe and comfort them, creating a sense of security and trust. Remember, your baby doesn't need expensive toys or elaborate activities; they simply crave your love and attention.

The postpartum period is a time of immense joy, but it's also a time of adjustment and challenges. By understanding the physical and emotional changes your partner is experiencing, actively participating in her care, and fostering a strong bond with your newborn, you can create a nurturing and supportive environment for your growing family.

Amidst the whirlwind of emotions and activity that follow childbirth, a sacred window of time opens—the Golden Hour. It's a fleeting yet precious interlude, a magical hour that sets the stage for a lifetime of bonding and connection between mother, baby, and father.

Picture this: The delivery room is abuzz with activity. Nurses scurry about, checking vital signs and tending to the new mother. But amidst the hustle and bustle, a quiet intimacy unfolds. The newborn, still slick with vernix and pulsating with life, is gently placed on their mother's bare chest. Skin-to-skin, heart-to-heart, a primal connection is forged.

This simple act, often overlooked in the excitement of the moment, is a cornerstone of early bonding. It's a symphony of touch, smell, and sound, a harmonious exchange of energy that transcends words. For the baby, it's a haven of warmth and security, a familiar heartbeat and scent that mimic the womb. For the mother, it's a moment of profound connection, a surge of oxytocin that reinforces her maternal instincts.

But the magic of the Golden Hour doesn't stop there. It's also a crucial time for breastfeeding initiation. As the baby rests on their mother's chest, their innate rooting and sucking reflexes kick in, guiding them towards the breast. This early initiation of breastfeeding not only provides essential nutrients and antibodies but also deepens the bond between mother and child.

For the father, the Golden Hour is an opportunity to participate in this intimate dance of connection. You can gently stroke your baby's skin, whisper words of love and welcome, and marvel at the miracle of life you've helped create. Your presence, your touch, and your voice can soothe and comfort your newborn, fostering a sense of security and trust.

I'll never forget the first time I held my daughter in my arms. She was so tiny, so fragile, yet so full of life. As I placed her on my wife's chest, I watched in awe as she instinctively nestled close, her tiny fingers grasping at her mother's skin. I gently stroked her soft hair, whispered words of love, and marveled at the tiny miracle we had created together.

In that moment, time seemed to stand still. The world outside the hospital room faded away, and all that mattered was the love and connection that blossomed between us and our daughter. It was a moment of pure magic, a memory that will forever be etched in my heart.

Skin-to-skin contact and breastfeeding are not just about physical nourishment. They're about emotional bonding, about creating a secure attachment that will lay the foundation for your child's future development. Studies have shown that babies who experience early skin-to-skin contact and breastfeeding are more likely to thrive both physically and emotionally. They have stronger immune systems, lower rates of infant mortality, and better cognitive and emotional development.

For mothers, skin-to-skin contact and breastfeeding can help reduce postpartum bleeding, promote uterine contraction, and lower the risk of postpartum depression. It can also enhance milk production and facilitate a successful breastfeeding relationship.

For fathers, participating in the Golden Hour can strengthen their bond with both their partner and their baby. It can help them feel more confident and involved in their role as a parent, and it can set the stage for a lifetime of love and connection with their child.

The Golden Hour is a fleeting moment, a precious gift that should be cherished and protected. It's a time to focus on your family, to celebrate the miracle of birth, and to create a foundation of love and trust that will last a lifetime. So, embrace this sacred time, hold your baby close, and let the magic unfold.

Postpartum Recovery: Caring for Your Partner and Bonding with Your Newborn.

The weeks following childbirth, a period often dubbed the "fourth trimester," are a whirlwind of emotions and physical adjustments. While the world outside celebrates the arrival of your newborn, your partner embarks on a personal journey of recovery and transformation. As a partner, understanding and supporting her during this vulnerable time is crucial, not just for her well-being, but also for the harmony and strength of your new family unit.

Postpartum recovery isn't a one-size-fits-all process. Every woman's experience is unique, shaped by factors such as the type of delivery, any complications, and her individual physiology. Some women bounce back quickly, while others may face lingering physical discomfort, emotional challenges, or even postpartum complications.

Understanding these varied experiences empowers you to offer tailored support. If your partner had a vaginal delivery, she might experience soreness in her perineal area, hemorrhoids, or constipation. A cesarean birth, on the other hand, brings its own set of challenges, including incisional pain, fatigue, and restrictions on lifting and physical activity.

In either case, your role as a partner is to be her advocate, her cheerleader, and her caretaker. Offer gentle encouragement and reassurance as she navigates the physical hurdles of recovery. Help with everyday tasks like changing diapers, preparing meals, and ensuring she stays hydrated. If she's experiencing discomfort, offer a warm bath, a gentle massage, or assistance with breastfeeding positions.

Rest and sleep are paramount during postpartum recovery. Sleep deprivation is a common challenge for new parents, but it's especially important for your partner to prioritize rest as her body heals. Encourage her to nap whenever possible, and take turns caring for the baby at night so she can get uninterrupted sleep.

Remember those early days after our daughter was born? We were both sleep-deprived zombies, stumbling through diaper changes and feedings in a haze of exhaustion. One night, after a particularly fussy feeding session, I gently took our daughter from my wife's arms and whispered, "Go get some rest, love. I've got her." The look of gratitude in her eyes as she drifted off to sleep was worth more than all the coffee in the world.

Nutrition also plays a vital role in postpartum recovery. A well-balanced diet rich in protein, iron, and vitamin C can help replenish energy levels, promote healing, and support milk production if your partner is breastfeeding. Offer to prepare nutritious meals and snacks, and stock the fridge with healthy options that are easy to grab on the go.

If she's breastfeeding, encourage her to stay hydrated and eat plenty of foods rich in omega-3 fatty acids, such as salmon, walnuts, and flaxseeds. These nutrients can help boost milk supply and support the baby's brain development.

Beyond the physical aspects of recovery, emotional support is equally important. The postpartum period can be an emotional rollercoaster, with fluctuating hormones and the overwhelming responsibility of caring for a newborn contributing to mood swings, anxiety, and even postpartum depression.

Be a listening ear, a safe space for your partner to express her feelings without judgment. Validate her emotions, reassure her that she's doing a great job, and remind her that you're in this together. If she's struggling with persistent sadness, anxiety, or feelings of hopelessness, encourage her to seek professional help. Postpartum depression is a treatable condition, and early intervention can make a significant difference in her well-being.

Supporting your partner through postpartum recovery is not just about practical tasks and emotional reassurance. It's also about celebrating her strength and resilience, acknowledging the incredible feat she's accomplished, and creating a loving and supportive environment where she can heal, bond with her baby, and rediscover her sense of self.

Chapter 8

Newborn Essentials: Caring for Your Baby

"A baby is born with a need to be loved - and never outgrows it." - Frank A. Clark

Welcoming a newborn into your life is like stepping into a magical, albeit sometimes chaotic, new world. Gone are the days of leisurely brunches and spontaneous road trips. Now, your life revolves around feeding schedules, diaper changes, and the sweet symphony of baby coos and cries. But amidst the whirlwind of new responsibilities, there's an undeniable joy in caring for your little one, a sense of purpose and fulfillment that transcends anything you've experienced before.

One of the first and most crucial aspects of caring for your newborn is feeding. Whether your partner chooses to breastfeed or formula feed, it's a task that requires patience, practice, and a whole lot of love. For breastfeeding mothers, establishing a good latch and ensuring adequate milk supply can be initial hurdles. As a supportive partner, you can offer encouragement, help with positioning, and make sure she's comfortable and well-nourished. If formula feeding is the chosen path, learning to prepare bottles, sterilize equipment, and pace feedings is essential. Remember, feeding time is not just about nourishment; it's an opportunity for bonding and creating a sense of security for your baby.

Diaper changes, another cornerstone of newborn care, might seem daunting at first. But with a little practice, you'll be a pro in no time. Gather your supplies – diapers, wipes, diaper cream, and a changing pad – and create a designated changing area that's safe and comfortable. Remember to always support your baby's head and neck, and be gentle when wiping their delicate skin.

Diaper changes are also a great opportunity for playful interaction, singing songs, making silly faces, and strengthening your bond with your little one.

Bath time can be a source of both joy and trepidation for new parents. While it's a chance to cleanse and refresh your baby, it's also a delicate task that requires a gentle touch and a watchful eye. Start with sponge baths until your baby's umbilical cord stump falls off, then gradually transition to tub baths. Use warm water and mild soap, and always support your baby's head and neck. Keep bath time short and sweet, and focus on creating a calm and enjoyable experience for both you and your baby.

Dressing a newborn can be a surprisingly intricate task, with tiny snaps, buttons, and zippers that seem to have a mind of their own. Choose soft, comfortable clothing made from natural fibers, and avoid anything with tight elastic or scratchy seams. Dress your baby in layers, as their body temperature can fluctuate easily. And don't forget the adorable accessories – hats, socks, and mittens can add a touch of personality and keep your little one warm and cozy.

Establishing sleep routines is another essential aspect of newborn care. Newborns sleep a lot, but their sleep patterns can be unpredictable, with frequent wakings for feedings and diaper changes. Creating a consistent bedtime routine, such as a warm bath, a gentle massage, and a soothing lullaby, can help signal to your baby that it's time to sleep.

As a new dad, sharing nighttime responsibilities is crucial for both your baby's well-being and your partner's rest. Offer to take turns with feedings, diaper changes, and soothing sessions. This not only allows your partner to get much-needed sleep, but it also strengthens your bond with your baby and fosters a sense of shared responsibility in parenting.

During those long nights, when sleep deprivation threatens to overwhelm you, remember that this phase is temporary. Your baby's sleep patterns will gradually become more predictable, and you'll both find a rhythm that works for your family. In the meantime, prioritize self-care, take naps when you can, and don't hesitate to ask for help from friends and family.

While caring for a newborn is a joyous experience, it's also important to be aware of common challenges that can arise. Colic, a condition characterized by excessive crying and fussiness, can be particularly distressing for both parents and baby. If your baby is experiencing colic, try soothing techniques such as swaddling, rocking, or offering a pacifier. White noise or gentle music can also be helpful.

Reflux, another common newborn issue, occurs when stomach acid flows back up into the esophagus, causing discomfort and spitting up. Keeping your baby upright after feedings, avoiding overfeeding, and burping frequently can help alleviate symptoms. If reflux persists or is severe, consult your pediatrician for further guidance.

Jaundice, a yellowing of the skin and eyes, is caused by a buildup of bilirubin in the blood. It's a common condition in newborns, but it usually resolves on its own within a few weeks. If jaundice is severe or persistent, your baby may need phototherapy, a treatment that uses light to break down bilirubin.

As a new dad, it's natural to feel overwhelmed or unsure of yourself when faced with these challenges. Remember, you're not alone. Millions of parents have navigated these same hurdles, and there are countless resources available to help you. Don't hesitate to reach out to your pediatrician, a lactation consultant, or a trusted friend or family member for advice and support.

Caring for a newborn is a journey of learning, growth, and endless love. It's a time of sleepless nights, endless diaper changes, and a rollercoaster of emotions. But amidst the chaos, there's also a profound sense of joy, connection, and wonder. By mastering the essentials of newborn care, sharing responsibilities with your partner, and navigating challenges with patience and resilience, you can create a nurturing and loving environment for your little one to thrive.

Feeding and Diapering: Mastering the Basics of Infant Care.

The first few weeks with your newborn are a delightful dance of love, exhaustion, and a steep learning curve as you and your partner master the intricate choreography of infant care. Two essential skills that will become your constant companions during this time are feeding and diapering. These may seem like simple tasks on the surface, but they form the bedrock of your baby's well-being. Mastering them not only ensures your little one's health and happiness but also bolsters your confidence as a new dad, transforming you from an eager apprentice to a capable caregiver.

Let's begin with feeding, the lifeblood of your baby's growth and development. It's a primal act, a symphony of nourishment and connection that lays the foundation for a lifetime of health and well-being. Whether your partner chooses the intimate path of breastfeeding or the practical route of formula feeding, your role as a supportive partner is crucial.

If breastfeeding is your chosen path, remember that it's a learning process for both mother and child. The early days can be a delicate dance, as your partner navigates the nuances of latching, milk supply, and the occasional bout of engorgement. Be her steadfast champion, offering words of encouragement, a helping hand with positioning, and a comforting presence that allows her to relax and focus on this sacred act.

Transform your living room into a tranquil oasis for breastfeeding, free from distractions and stress. Fluff the pillows, dim the lights, and maybe even put on some soothing music. Offer to bring her a glass of water, a healthy snack, or anything else she might need to feel comfortable and nourished. And don't forget to learn the art of burping your baby after feedings – a gentle pat on the back can work wonders in releasing trapped air and preventing discomfort.

If circumstances lead you to formula feeding, embrace it with confidence. Modern formulas are meticulously designed to provide all the essential nutrients your baby needs to thrive. Choose a formula that's appropriate for your baby's age and any specific dietary considerations, and follow the preparation instructions diligently.

Sterilizing bottles and nipples, meticulously measuring formula, and warming it to the perfect temperature might feel like a science experiment at first, but you'll soon develop a rhythm that feels second nature. Remember, every bottle you prepare is an act of love, a testament to your dedication to your baby's well-being.

Whether breast or bottle, feeding time is more than just sustenance; it's a precious opportunity to forge a deep connection with your little one. Cradle your baby close, gaze into their eyes, and speak softly to them. Your voice, your touch, your presence — these are the building blocks of a bond that will last a lifetime.

Now, let's turn our attention to the other constant in a newborn's life: diapers. Yes, they're messy, they're smelly, and they require frequent attention. But they're also a testament to your baby's growth and a chance to practice your newfound caregiving skills.

Before you embark on your first diaper change, gather your supplies like a seasoned adventurer preparing for an expedition. You'll need a stockpile of diapers, a trusty pack of wipes, a soothing diaper cream, and a designated changing area that's both safe and comfortable.

When duty calls, lay your baby on the changing pad and gently remove the soiled diaper. Use wipes to clean their bottom thoroughly, taking care to wipe from front to back to prevent infections. Apply a thin layer of diaper cream to create a protective barrier against irritation. Then, slide a fresh diaper under your baby, ensuring a snug but not too tight fit.

Note, diaper changes are more than just a chore. They're a chance to interact with your baby, to sing silly songs, make funny faces, and shower them with love and affection. It's in these everyday moments that the magic of parenthood truly unfolds.

As you gain experience, you'll develop your own diaper-changing style. Some dads prefer a standing approach, while others find a seated position more comfortable. Don't be afraid to experiment and find what works best for you and your baby.

And remember, practice makes perfect. The first few diaper changes might be a bit messy, but with time and patience, you'll become a diaper-changing maestro, able to handle any situation with grace and a touch of humor.

Feeding and diapering are just the beginning of your journey as a caregiver. Embrace these tasks with an open heart and a willingness to learn, and you'll not only ensure your baby's well-being but also create cherished memories and strengthen your bond with your little one.

Sleep, that elusive elixir of rejuvenation, takes on a whole new meaning in the realm of newborn parenting. As the sun dips below the horizon, painting the sky in hues of orange and purple, a symphony of coos, whimpers, and cries fills the air. Your once-peaceful nights transform into a whirlwind of feedings, diaper changes, and desperate attempts to soothe your little one back to slumber. Sleep deprivation becomes your constant companion, a relentless fog that clouds your mind and challenges your patience. But amidst the exhaustion, there's a glimmer of hope: establishing routines and mastering the art of soothing can help you and your baby find a harmonious rhythm, even in the midst of the sleepless storm.

The first step in this quest for peaceful nights is understanding your baby's sleep patterns. Newborns, with their tiny stomachs and developing circadian rhythms, sleep in short bursts, waking frequently for nourishment and comfort. It's a far cry from the eight-hour stretches you might have enjoyed pre-parenthood, but it's perfectly normal and essential for their growth and development.

Embrace the concept of "cluster feeding," where your baby feeds frequently for several hours in the evening, often referred to as the "witching hour." This helps them tank up for longer stretches of sleep at night. Be patient, be present, and offer your little one the comfort and nourishment they crave.

As your baby grows, you'll start to notice patterns in their sleep-wake cycle. This is where establishing a consistent bedtime routine can work wonders. Think of it as a gentle lullaby for your baby's senses, signaling that it's time to wind down and prepare for sleep.

A warm bath, a gentle massage, a quiet story, or a soft lullaby can all be part of your bedtime ritual. Keep the environment calm and dimly lit, and avoid stimulating activities before bed. By repeating this routine each night, you'll help your baby associate these cues with sleep, making bedtime transitions smoother and more predictable.

Consistency is key. Stick to the same routine as much as possible, even on weekends or when you're traveling. This helps regulate your baby's internal clock and promotes healthy sleep habits.

Creating a sleep-conducive environment is also essential. Keep the room cool, dark, and quiet. Use blackout curtains or blinds to block out light, and consider using a white noise machine to mask disruptive sounds. Dress your baby in comfortable sleepwear, and make sure their crib or bassinet is safe and free of any loose blankets or pillows.

Swaddling, an age-old technique of wrapping your baby snugly in a blanket, can also be helpful in promoting sleep. It mimics the feeling of being in the womb, providing a sense of security and comfort. However, it's important to swaddle correctly to ensure your baby's safety.

As a new dad, sharing nighttime responsibilities with your partner is not only an act of love and support, but also a practical necessity. Sleep deprivation can take a toll on both of you, affecting your mood, energy levels, and overall well-being.

Offer to take turns with nighttime feedings, diaper changes, and soothing sessions. This allows your partner to get some much-needed rest, while also strengthening your bond with your baby. If your partner is breastfeeding, you can still play an active role by bringing her the baby, burping them afterward, and helping them settle back to sleep.

Those early weeks with my daughter, when the nights seemed endless and the days blurred together in a haze of exhaustion. My wife and I quickly learned the importance of teamwork, taking turns with nighttime duties so we could both get some semblance of rest.

One particularly challenging night, my wife was struggling to soothe our fussy daughter. I gently took the baby from her arms, cradled her close, and started humming a lullaby. As I rocked her back and forth, I felt a sense of peace and connection wash over me. In that moment, I realized the profound power of a father's love, and the importance of sharing the joys and challenges of parenthood with my partner.

While establishing routines and sharing responsibilities can go a long way in managing sleep deprivation, there will inevitably be nights when your baby is inconsolable or struggling to settle. This is where the art of soothing comes into play.

Every baby is different, and what works for one may not work for another. Experiment with different techniques, such as rocking, swaying, singing, or offering a pacifier. White noise, gentle music, or even the rhythmic sound of your heartbeat can also be soothing.

Remember, patience is key. Some nights, it might take a while for your baby to settle. Don't get discouraged, and don't be afraid to ask for help if you need it. Reach out to your pediatrician, a lactation consultant, or a trusted friend or family member for advice and support.

In addition to sleep challenges, newborns can also experience other common issues, such as colic, reflux, and jaundice. Colic, characterized by excessive crying and fussiness, can be particularly frustrating for new parents. While the exact cause is unknown, it's believed to be related to digestive discomfort or an immature nervous system.

If your baby is experiencing colic, try soothing techniques such as swaddling, carrying them in a baby carrier, or offering a warm bath. Gentle massage, white noise, and rhythmic movement can also be helpful. Remember, colic is usually temporary and will eventually subside.

Reflux, another common newborn issue, occurs when stomach acid flows back up into the esophagus, causing discomfort and spitting up. Keeping your baby upright after feedings, avoiding overfeeding, and burping frequently can help alleviate symptoms. If reflux persists or is severe, consult your pediatrician for further guidance.

Jaundice, a yellowing of the skin and eyes, is caused by a buildup of bilirubin in the blood. It's a common condition in newborns, but it usually resolves on its own within a few weeks. If jaundice is severe or persistent, your baby may need phototherapy, a treatment that uses light to break down bilirubin.

You're not alone in navigating these challenges. Millions of parents have faced similar hurdles, and there's a wealth of resources and support available. Don't hesitate to reach out to your pediatrician, a lactation consultant, or other trusted professionals for guidance.

As you journey through the early days of parenthood, remember that every sleepless night, every diaper change, and every soothing session is an opportunity to bond with your baby and create a foundation of love and trust that will last a lifetime. Embrace the challenges, celebrate the triumphs, and cherish the precious moments, for they are fleeting and irreplaceable.

Chapter 9

The Fourth Trimester: Adjusting to Parenthood

"The fourth trimester is not a myth. It's a continuation of the profound transformation that began with pregnancy, a sacred space where you and your partner learn the intricate dance of parenthood." *-Anonymouse*

While the birth of your baby marks a joyous milestone, it's also the beginning of a new chapter filled with both exhilaration and exhaustion. The fourth trimester, the often-overlooked period spanning the first three months after childbirth, is a time of profound adjustment for both parents. It's a delicate dance of recovery, bonding, and navigating the uncharted waters of new parenthood.

For the new mother, the fourth trimester is a symphony of physical and emotional changes. Her body is healing from the physical demands of childbirth, hormones are fluctuating, and sleep deprivation is a constant companion. She may experience a range of emotions, from elation and wonder to anxiety, sadness, and even postpartum depression.

"The first few weeks after my son was born were a blur," recalls new dad, Alex. "My wife was amazing, but I could see the exhaustion in her eyes. She was juggling breastfeeding, sleepless nights, and the emotional rollercoaster of new motherhood. I tried to be as supportive as possible, taking on as much as I could around the house and encouraging her to rest whenever she could."

As a partner, your role during this period is to be a pillar of strength, offering unwavering support and understanding. Start by acknowledging the enormity of what your partner has just accomplished. Bringing a new life into the world is a feat of strength and resilience, and she deserves your admiration and gratitude.

Be patient with her as she navigates the physical and emotional challenges of postpartum recovery. Offer gentle encouragement, listen without judgment, and provide a safe space for her to express her feelings. Remember, she's not just recovering from childbirth; she's also adjusting to a new identity as a mother.

"I remember feeling a bit helpless at times," shares another new dad, Ben. "My wife was so focused on the baby, and I didn't want to intrude or overwhelm her. But I also wanted to be involved and supportive. I started by doing small things, like bringing her snacks and water, changing diapers, and giving her a break to shower or nap. It made a world of difference for both of us."

Practical support is key during the fourth trimester. Take on household chores, prepare meals, and run errands so your partner can focus on resting and bonding with the baby. Offer to take the night shift, allowing her to get some much-needed sleep. Even small gestures, like bringing her a cup of tea or offering a foot rub, can go a long way in showing your love and support.

In addition to physical recovery, postpartum mental health is a critical concern. The "baby blues," characterized by mood swings, anxiety, and tearfulness, are common in the first few weeks after childbirth. However, if these symptoms persist or worsen, it could be a sign of postpartum depression, a more serious condition that requires professional help.

Be vigilant for signs of postpartum depression, such as persistent sadness, loss of interest in activities, changes in appetite or sleep patterns, and difficulty bonding with the baby. If you notice any of these symptoms, encourage your partner to seek help from a healthcare professional. Remember, there's no shame in asking for help, and early intervention can make a significant difference in her recovery.

Amidst the challenges of the fourth trimester, don't forget to embrace the joy of bonding with your newborn. This is a precious time to establish a deep and lasting connection with your child, one that will shape their development and your relationship for years to come.

Engage in skin-to-skin contact, holding your baby close and allowing them to feel the warmth of your body and the rhythm of your heartbeat. Talk, sing, and read to your baby, even if they don't understand the words yet. Your voice and presence will soothe and comfort them, creating a sense of security and trust.

Playtime is another essential way to bond with your baby. Make silly faces, tickle their toes, and engage in gentle games of peek-a-boo. These interactions not only foster a sense of joy and connection, but also stimulate your baby's brain development and lay the foundation for future learning.

As your baby grows, continue to nurture their development through reading, singing, and exploring the world around them. Point out different colors and shapes, describe the sounds you hear, and encourage them to reach for and grasp objects. These simple interactions can have a profound impact on your baby's cognitive, social, and emotional growth.

Co-parenting is another crucial aspect of navigating the fourth trimester and beyond. It's about working together as a team, sharing responsibilities, and supporting each other's parenting styles. Establishing a shared philosophy early on can help prevent misunderstandings and conflicts down the road.

"My wife and I had different ideas about sleep training," recalls Alex. "She was more inclined towards a gentle approach, while I was worried about creating bad habits. We had a few heated discussions, but eventually, we found a middle ground that worked for both of us and our baby."

Open and honest communication is key to successful co-parenting. Talk about your expectations, fears, and hopes for your parenting journey. Be willing to compromise and find solutions that meet both of your needs. Remember, there's no one right way to parent, and the best approach is one that feels right for your family.

The fourth trimester is a time of immense change and adjustment. It's a period of healing, bonding, and discovering the rhythms of your new family. By supporting your partner, fostering a connection with your baby, and establishing a strong co-parenting foundation, you can navigate this transformative time with grace and resilience, setting the stage for a lifetime of love, laughter, and shared experiences.

Emotional Rollercoaster: Understanding Postpartum Emotions and Seeking Support.

In the quiet moments following the whirlwind of childbirth, a new reality sets in. As the adrenaline fades and the hospital room empties, leaving you alone with your partner and your newborn, a wave of emotions washes over you both. Joy, exhaustion, awe, and a touch of disbelief mingle in a complex tapestry. While these feelings are all part of the beautiful tapestry of new parenthood, it's crucial to recognize that the postpartum period can also be a time of emotional turbulence, particularly for the new mother.

The term *"baby blues"* often gets tossed around lightly, but it's a real phenomenon affecting up to 80% of new mothers. Picture this: one moment, she's gazing at your baby with boundless love, and the next, she's overcome with tears, anxiety, or a sense of overwhelming sadness. These mood swings, often accompanied by irritability, insomnia, and difficulty concentrating, are a normal response to the hormonal fluctuations, sleep deprivation, and the sheer magnitude of adjusting to motherhood.

But sometimes, the baby blues linger, morphing into something more profound and persistent. Postpartum depression (PPD) affects approximately 1 in 7 women, casting a shadow over what should be a joyous time. It's characterized by feelings of sadness, hopelessness, and worthlessness that last for weeks or even months. It can interfere with a mother's ability to care for herself and her baby, and it can strain relationships and disrupt family life.

As a partner, recognizing the signs of postpartum depression is crucial. If your partner exhibits any of the following symptoms for more than two weeks, it's essential to seek professional help:

- Persistent sadness, anxiety, or emptiness

- Loss of interest or pleasure in activities she once enjoyed

- Changes in appetite or sleep patterns

- Difficulty bonding with the baby

- Feelings of guilt, worthlessness, or hopelessness

- Thoughts of harming herself or the baby

Remember, postpartum depression is not a character flaw or a sign of weakness. It's a treatable medical condition, and seeking help is a sign of strength and courage. Encourage your partner to talk to her healthcare provider, a therapist, or a support group. Offer your unwavering support and understanding, and remind her that she's not alone in this journey.

But postpartum emotional challenges aren't limited to mothers. Fathers, too, can experience a range of emotions during this time. The transition to parenthood can trigger anxiety, stress, and even feelings of inadequacy. The sleepless nights, the constant demands of a newborn, and the shifting dynamics of your relationship can all contribute to emotional strain.

It's important for dads to acknowledge and express their own feelings, rather than bottling them up. Talk to your partner, a trusted friend, or a therapist about what you're going through. Remember, seeking support is not a sign of weakness, but a testament to your commitment to your own well-being and the health of your family.

Creating a supportive and nurturing environment at home is essential for both parents during the postpartum period. This means prioritizing rest, healthy eating, and gentle exercise. It also means carving out time for self-care, even if it's just a few minutes each day to meditate, read a book, or take a walk.

Remember those date nights you enjoyed before the baby arrived? While they might look a little different now, it's still important to make time for each other as a couple. Schedule a babysitter, order takeout, and enjoy a quiet evening together. Even a simple walk in the park or a shared cup of coffee can help you reconnect and strengthen your bond.

Open and honest communication is another key ingredient in navigating the emotional rollercoaster of postpartum life. Talk to your partner about how you're both feeling, share your concerns and anxieties, and celebrate your victories, no matter how small. You're in this together, and by supporting each other, you can weather any storm.

Finally, don't hesitate to seek outside support if needed. Many communities offer postpartum support groups, parenting classes, and resources for new parents. Connecting with other parents who are going through similar experiences can provide a sense of community, validation, and practical advice.

The fourth trimester is a time of profound change and adjustment. It's a journey filled with both challenges and immense rewards. By acknowledging and addressing the emotional rollercoaster of new parenthood, seeking support when needed, and prioritizing self-care and connection, you can create a nurturing and resilient family unit, ready to embrace the joys and challenges of raising your little one.

Play is the universal language of childhood, a gateway to joy, learning, and emotional connection. It's through play that your baby explores the world, develops essential skills, and discovers the sheer delight of being alive. As a new dad, embracing the playful spirit of your child can unlock a treasure trove of shared experiences and strengthen your bond in ways you never imagined.

Remember, play doesn't need to be complicated or expensive. The simplest interactions can spark a symphony of giggles and smiles. Make silly faces, blow raspberries on their tummy, or engage in a game of peek-a-boo. These lighthearted moments not only bring joy to your baby but also foster a sense of trust and security, knowing that you're there to share in their delight.

As your baby grows, so too will the possibilities for play. Tummy time, rolling a ball back and forth, stacking blocks, and singing silly songs are all wonderful ways to engage with your little one and encourage their development. These playful interactions stimulate their senses, strengthen their muscles, and spark their curiosity about the world around them.

Reading aloud to your baby, even from the earliest days, is a gift that keeps on giving. It's a chance to cuddle up close, share the warmth of your voice, and introduce them to the magic of stories. Choose books with bright colors, simple patterns, and engaging textures. Use different voices and inflections to bring the characters to life, and don't be afraid to get silly and animated.

As your baby grows, expand your library to include a variety of genres and styles. From classic fairy tales to interactive board books, reading together creates a cozy and intimate space for bonding, nurturing a lifelong love of learning. It's also a wonderful way to wind down before bedtime, establishing a calming routine that signals to your baby that it's time to rest.

Beyond play and reading, there are countless ways to engage with your baby and create lasting memories. Sing lullabies, dance around the living room, take walks in the park, and explore the world together. Be present in the moment, put away your phone, and give your baby your undivided attention.

Remember, your baby doesn't need fancy toys or elaborate outings to feel loved and connected. They simply crave your presence, your touch, and your voice. By actively engaging with your baby and responding to their cues, you're not only fostering their development but also creating a treasure trove of memories that will be cherished for years to come.

As your baby grows and develops, so too will your bond. Each milestone, from their first smile to their first steps, is a testament to the love and care you've poured into their lives. It's a reminder of the incredible journey you're on together, a journey filled with joy, challenges, and the boundless potential of a parent-child relationship.

Embrace the messy moments, the sleepless nights, and the overwhelming love that comes with fatherhood. It's a role that will challenge you, transform you, and ultimately reward you in ways you never imagined. By actively participating in your baby's life, you're not just building a strong bond; you're creating a legacy of love that will echo through generations.

Chapter 10

Navigating the First Year: Milestones and Challenges

"The first year of a child's life is a magical journey, a symphony of growth and discovery that unfolds at an astonishing pace." Anonymous

Did you know that a baby's brain grows by an astounding 175% in the first year of life? This remarkable development sets the stage for a symphony of milestones, each a testament to your little one's blossoming potential. As a father, witnessing and nurturing this growth is a privilege and a joy, but it also comes with its fair share of challenges. Understanding the key developmental milestones and anticipating common hurdles can empower you to provide the support and guidance your baby needs to thrive during this transformative year.

Let's embark on a journey through the first year, exploring the remarkable milestones that await your little one, as well as the challenges you might encounter along the way.

In the first few months, your baby's primary focus is on physical development. They'll gradually gain control of their head, neck, and limbs, learning to lift their head, roll over, and eventually sit up with support. Their senses will sharpen, and they'll begin to explore the world through touch, sight, sound, taste, and smell.

Encourage your baby's physical development by providing plenty of opportunities for movement and exploration. Tummy time, for example, helps strengthen their neck and back muscles, preparing them for crawling and walking. Offer age-appropriate toys that encourage reaching, grasping, and exploring different textures. And don't forget the power of touch – gentle massages, cuddles, and skin-to-skin contact can foster a sense of security and promote healthy development.

As your baby's physical skills improve, so too will their cognitive abilities. They'll start to recognize familiar faces and voices, track moving objects with their eyes, and respond to their name. They'll also begin to babble and coo, experimenting with sounds and language.

Encourage your baby's cognitive development by talking, singing, and reading to them frequently. Describe the world around them, point out different colors and shapes, and engage them in simple games and activities. Offer a variety of age-appropriate toys that stimulate their senses and encourage exploration.

Social-emotional development is another crucial aspect of your baby's first year. They'll begin to express a range of emotions, from joy and excitement to sadness and frustration. They'll also start to develop a sense of self and form attachments to their primary caregivers.

Foster your baby's social-emotional development by responding sensitively to their cues. Offer comfort when they're upset, celebrate their achievements, and provide a safe and nurturing environment where they feel loved and valued. Encourage social interaction by introducing them to other babies and caregivers, and model positive behaviors like kindness, empathy, and respect.

As your baby grows and develops, they'll encounter various challenges along the way. Teething, for example, can be a painful and frustrating experience for both baby and parents. Offer teething toys, cold compresses, and gentle massages to soothe their gums. If your baby is particularly fussy, talk to your pediatrician about safe pain relief options.

Separation anxiety, a common developmental milestone, typically emerges around six to eight months of age. Your baby may become clingy and upset when separated from their primary caregivers. This is a normal phase, but it can be challenging for parents. Reassure your baby that you'll always return, and offer comfort and reassurance when they're feeling anxious.

Sleep disruptions are another common challenge during the first year. As your baby's sleep patterns evolve, they may experience periods of wakefulness or difficulty settling down at night. Establishing consistent bedtime routines, creating a calm sleep environment, and offering gentle comfort can help your baby develop healthy sleep habits.

Introducing solid foods is an exciting milestone, usually occurring around six months of age. Start with single-ingredient purees, such as fruits, vegetables, or cereals, and gradually introduce new flavors and textures. Be patient and observant, watching for signs of allergies or sensitivities.

Remember, every baby develops at their own pace. Don't compare your child to others or feel pressured to rush milestones. Celebrate each achievement, no matter how small, and cherish the unique journey of your baby's first year.

By understanding the key developmental milestones, anticipating common challenges, and providing unwavering love and support, you can create a nurturing environment where your baby can thrive. The first year is a whirlwind of growth and discovery, a testament to the resilience of the human spirit and the boundless love between parent and child.

Developmental Milestones: Tracking Your Baby's Growth and Development.

As a new dad, you're about to embark on an incredible journey watching your little one grow and change at a remarkable pace. The first year of your baby's life is packed with astounding developments that will leave you in awe. Let's dive into the key milestones you can expect and how to support your child's growth along the way.

From the moment your baby arrives, they're primed for rapid development. In just 12 short months, your newborn will transform from a tiny, dependent bundle into an increasingly mobile, communicative, and curious little person. While every child develops at their own pace, understanding typical milestones can help you celebrate your baby's progress and identify any potential concerns early on.

Physical Development: In the early weeks, your baby's physical abilities are limited, but they're laying the groundwork for future skills. Initially, your newborn will have jerky, uncontrolled movements and a strong grasp reflex. By 2-3 months, you'll notice improved head control when held upright. Around 4 months, many babies can roll from tummy to back, with back-to-tummy rolls following a month or two later.

The 6-month mark often brings exciting changes. Your baby may be sitting unsupported for short periods, reaching for objects with improved coordination, and possibly starting to scoot or crawl. By 9 months, many babies are masters at sitting and may be pulling themselves up to stand while holding onto furniture. Walking usually emerges between 9-18 months, with the average age being around 12 months.

Fine motor skills also develop rapidly. Your 3-month-old may start batting at hanging toys, while a 6-month-old can often transfer objects from hand to hand. By 9 months, the *"pincer grasp"* emerges, allowing your baby to pick up small objects between thumb and forefinger – a skill that's crucial for self-feeding and exploration.

Cognitive Development: Your baby's brain is like a sponge, constantly absorbing information from their environment. In the first few months, your little one will start to recognize familiar faces and voices. By 3-4 months, many babies show a preference for novelty, becoming more interested in new toys or faces.

Around 6 months, object permanence begins to develop. Your baby starts to understand that objects continue to exist even when out of sight. This is why peek-a-boo becomes endlessly entertaining! By 9 months, many babies can follow simple commands like "wave bye-bye" and understand the concept of cause and effect.

Problem-solving skills emerge as your baby approaches their first birthday. You might see them figuring out how to reach a toy that's slightly out of grasp or how to fit shapes into a sorter. Their memory is also improving, allowing them to recall where favorite toys are hidden or to anticipate routines.

Language Development: While your baby won't be reciting Shakespeare anytime soon, language development starts from day one. Newborns communicate through cries and coos, but by 2-3 months, you'll hear more varied vocalizations. Around 4-6 months, many babies begin to babble, stringing together consonant-vowel sounds like "ba-ba" or "ma-ma."

By 9 months, your baby may understand simple words like "no" and "bye-bye." Many babies say their first recognizable word around their first birthday, though some are earlier or later. Receptive language (understanding) develops faster than expressive language (speaking), so don't be surprised if your 1-year-old can follow simple instructions even if they're not talking much yet.

Social and Emotional Development: Your baby's social skills blossom throughout the first year. Newborns are hardwired to prefer human faces and voices. By 2 months, most babies reward their parents with their first social smiles. Around 4-6 months, you'll hear delightful belly laughs and see your baby's personality emerging.

The concept of stranger anxiety often appears around 6-8 months. Your previously social butterfly may suddenly become wary of unfamiliar faces. This is a normal developmental stage that shows your baby can distinguish between familiar and unfamiliar people.

As your baby approaches their first birthday, you'll see more intentional social behaviors. They may offer toys to others, wave goodbye, or play simple games like pat-a-cake. They're also becoming more aware of others' emotions and may try to comfort someone who seems upset.

Supporting Your Baby's Development: As a dad, you play a crucial role in fostering your baby's growth. Here are some ways to support your little one's development:

1. Engage in plenty of face-to-face interaction. Talk, sing, and read to your baby from day one. This not only supports language development but also strengthens your bond.

2. Provide a safe environment for exploration. As your baby becomes mobile, ensure your home is babyproofed so they can safely discover their world.

3. Offer age-appropriate toys and activities. Simple household items often make the best toys — a plastic

cup and spoon can provide endless entertainment for a 6-month-old.

4. Encourage tummy time from early on. This helps strengthen neck, shoulder, and arm muscles, preparing your baby for crawling and other milestones.

5. Respond consistently to your baby's cues. This helps them feel secure and lays the foundation for healthy emotional development.

6. Get moving together. As your baby grows, incorporate physical play like gentle bouncing or assisted "walking" to support gross motor development.

7. Establish routines. Consistent schedules for feeding, sleeping, and play can help your baby feel secure and aid in cognitive development.

Every baby is unique. While it's helpful to be aware of typical milestones, try not to get caught up in comparisons. Some babies may reach certain milestones earlier or later than average, and that's usually perfectly normal.

A study published in the journal "Pediatrics" found that only 4% of children achieve all milestones at the exact ages outlined in standard milestone checklists. This underscores the wide range of normal development.

If you have concerns about your baby's development, don't hesitate to discuss them with your pediatrician. Early intervention can make a significant difference if there are any developmental delays. Generally, pediatricians look for the following red flags:

- No babbling, pointing, or other gestures by 12 months

- No single words by 16 months

- No two-word phrases by 24 months

- Any loss of previously acquired speech or social skills

It's worth noting that premature babies may hit milestones later than full-term infants. A general rule of thumb is to use your baby's adjusted age (calculated from their due date rather than birth date) when considering milestones for the first two years.

As you track your baby's progress, consider keeping a journal or using a baby milestone app. This can be a wonderful keepsake and a useful reference for pediatrician visits. Many dads find it rewarding to document their baby's "firsts" – first smile, first laugh, first steps. These memories are precious and can fly by in the whirlwind of new parenthood.

Watching your baby grow and develop is one of the most rewarding aspects of fatherhood. Each new skill your little one masters is a cause for celebration. From that first toothless grin to those wobbly first steps, every milestone is a testament to your baby's incredible journey of growth and learning.

Remember, your consistent love, attention, and support are the most crucial factors in your baby's development. By being present and engaged, you're giving your child the best possible start in life. Embrace this amazing year of firsts, knowing that you're playing a vital role in shaping your child's future. The sleepless nights and dirty diapers will pass, but the memories of your baby's first year will last a lifetime.

Common Challenges: Dealing with Colic, Teething, and Sleep Regressions.

As a new dad, you've made it through pregnancy, birth, and the first few months. You might be thinking the tough part is over. Well, I've got news for you – the adventure is just beginning. The first year of your baby's life is filled with incredible moments of joy, but it also comes with its fair share of challenges. Let's dive into some of the hurdles you might face and how to handle them like a pro.

Colic: The Crying Conundrum

Picture this: It's 2 AM, and your baby has been crying for what feels like an eternity. You've fed them, changed them, and rocked them, but nothing seems to work. Welcome to the world of colic.

Colic affects about 20-25% of babies, typically starting around 2-3 weeks of age and peaking at 6-8 weeks. It's characterized by intense, inconsolable crying for at least three hours a day, three days a week, for three weeks or more. The cause? Well, that's the million-dollar question. Theories range from an immature digestive system to overstimulation, but the truth is, we don't know for sure.

As a dad, dealing with a colicky baby can be incredibly frustrating and emotionally draining. You might feel helpless or even start to doubt your parenting abilities. Rest assured, you're not alone, and this too shall pass.

Here are some strategies to help you cope:

1. The 5 S's: Pediatrician Harvey Karp's method involves Swaddling, Side/Stomach position, Shushing, Swinging, and Sucking. Many dads swear by this technique.

2. Motion is lotion: Take your baby for a car ride or a walk in the stroller. The movement can be soothing.

3. White noise: A fan, vacuum cleaner, or white noise app can sometimes work wonders.

4. Infant massage: Gentle tummy rubs may help relieve gas and discomfort.

5. Tag team with your partner: Take shifts so you both can get some rest.

Colic is temporary. Most cases resolve by 3-4 months. In the meantime, don't hesitate to reach out to your pediatrician or a support group for colicky babies. Sometimes, just knowing you're not alone can make a world of difference.

Teething: When Gums Attack

Just when you think you've got this parenting thing figured out, your baby starts drooling excessively, chewing on everything in sight, and waking up at night in discomfort. Congratulations, you've entered the teething phase!

Most babies start teething between 4-7 months, but some can begin as early as 3 months or as late as 12 months. On average, babies will have about 6-8 teeth by their first birthday. The process can be uncomfortable for your little one, leading to irritability, disrupted sleep, and loss of appetite.

For dad, your mission is to provide comfort and relief. Here's your teething toolkit:

1. Chilled teething rings: Pop them in the fridge (not the freezer) for extra soothing power.

2. Frozen washcloth: Wet one end, freeze it, and let your baby gnaw on it.

3. Gum massage: Use a clean finger to gently rub your baby's gums.

4. Teething biscuits: For babies over 6 months, these can provide relief (and a mess to clean up).

5. Over-the-counter pain relief: Consult your pediatrician about using acetaminophen or ibuprofen for severe discomfort.

Be cautious of teething necklaces or bracelets, as they pose a choking hazard. Also, avoid topical numbing gels, as they can be harmful if swallowed.

Pro tip: Keep a few extra shirts handy for yourself. The teething phase comes with an abundance of drool, and you'll likely end up wearing some of it.

Sleep Regressions: When Z's Become A's (for Awake)

You've finally established a decent sleep routine, and your baby is sleeping for longer stretches. Life is good. Then suddenly, your little one starts waking up every hour, fighting naps, and turning bedtime into a battleground. Welcome to sleep regressions.

Sleep regressions typically occur at 4 months, 8-10 months, and 18 months, though some babies experience them at different times. They're often linked to developmental milestones and usually last 2-6 weeks.

The 4-month sleep regression is particularly notorious. It coincides with significant changes in your baby's sleep cycles, as they transition from newborn sleep patterns to more adult-like ones. This can lead to more frequent night wakings and shorter naps.

Here's how you can help your family weather the storm:

1. Stick to your routine: Consistency is key. Maintain your bedtime rituals and nap schedules as much as possible.

2. Create a sleep-friendly environment: Keep the room dark, cool, and quiet. Consider using blackout curtains and a white noise machine.

3. Gradually extend awake times: As your baby grows, they may need longer wake windows between naps.

4. Practice independent sleep skills: If you haven't already, start putting your baby down drowsy but awake.

5. Be patient and flexible: Remember, this is a phase. Be willing to adjust

your expectations and strategies as needed.

6. Support your partner: Take turns with night wakings if possible, especially if your partner is breastfeeding.

A study published in the journal Sleep found that infants who followed consistent bedtime routines fell asleep faster, woke less during the night, and slept for longer overall. So, while it might be tempting to throw routines out the window during a regression, try to stay the course.

The Importance of Self-Care

Dealing with these challenges can be exhausting, both physically and emotionally. It's crucial to take care of yourself too. A study in the Journal of Child and Family Studies found that fathers who practiced self-care reported lower stress levels and better relationships with their children.

Make time for exercise, even if it's just a 15-minute walk. Stay connected with friends and family. Don't be afraid to ask for help when you need it. Remember, taking care of yourself isn't selfish – it's essential for being the best dad you can be.

Bonding Through Challenges

While these hurdles can be tough, they also present unique opportunities for bonding with your baby. During a colicky episode, your calm presence and soothing voice can be incredibly comforting. When your baby is teething, your gentle gum massage might provide the relief they need. And during sleep regressions, those middle-of-the-night cuddles, while exhausting, can be precious moments of connection.

A study in the journal Attachment & Human Development found that fathers who were actively involved in soothing their infants during times of distress reported stronger emotional bonds with their children later on.

The Power of Perspective

While you navigate these challenges, try to maintain a broader perspective. Each phase is temporary, even if it doesn't feel like it in the moment. Your baby is growing, developing, and learning at an incredible rate. These challenges are often side effects of exciting developmental leaps.

For instance, the 8-10 month sleep regression often coincides with major physical milestones like crawling and pulling up to stand. Your baby's brain is so excited about these new skills that it has trouble shutting off at night. Frustrating? Absolutely. But also pretty amazing when you think about it.

Celebrate the Small Victories

In the midst of these challenges, don't forget to celebrate the small victories. Did your colicky baby have a good stretch of quiet time today? Victory! Did your teething baby manage to nap for more than 20 minutes? Time for a silent dad dance! Did everyone in the house get four consecutive hours of sleep during a regression? Break out the confetti (quietly, of course).

Keeping a sense of humor and acknowledging these small wins can help you maintain a positive outlook during tough times.

Looking Ahead

As your baby approaches their first birthday, you'll likely find that many of these early challenges have eased. The colicky crying has subsided, those first few teeth have come through, and sleep has (hopefully) become more predictable.

But don't get too comfortable – toddlerhood brings its own set of adventures. Tantrums, picky eating, and the terrible twos are just around the corner. But guess what? You've got this. The resilience, problem-solving skills, and patience you've developed during this first year have prepared you for whatever comes next.

Remember, every challenge you face is helping you become a better, more confident dad. You're not just surviving these hurdles – you're learning, growing, and bonding with your child in the process.

So the next time you find yourself pacing the floor with a crying baby at 3 AM, or changing your shirt for the fifth time due to teething drool, or staring bleary-eyed at the baby monitor during a sleep regression, take a deep breath and remind yourself: "I've got this. I'm becoming the dad my child needs me to be."

Chapter 11

Balancing Fatherhood and Your Life

"The moment a child is born, the father is also born. He never existed before. The man existed, but the father, never. A father is something absolutely new." - Rajneesh

The transition to fatherhood is a profound journey that reshapes your identity, priorities, and daily life. While the focus is often on the new baby, it's crucial to recognize that you, as a father, are also undergoing a significant transformation. This chapter delves into the art of balancing your new role as a dad with the other aspects of your life, ensuring that you not only survive but thrive in this new chapter.

Recent studies have shown that nearly 10% of new fathers experience postpartum depression, a statistic that underscores the importance of prioritizing your mental health as you step into fatherhood. The demands of caring for a newborn, coupled with sleep deprivation and the pressure to "have it all together," can take a toll on your well-being. Recognizing this, it's essential to develop strategies for self-care and stress management that fit into your new lifestyle.

One effective approach is to carve out small pockets of time for yourself throughout the day. This might mean waking up 15 minutes earlier to enjoy a quiet cup of coffee, or using your lunch break at work to take a brisk walk. These moments, while brief, can provide much-needed respite and help you recharge. Remember, self-care isn't selfish – it's necessary for being the best father you can be.

Physical exercise is another crucial component of self-care that often falls by the wayside for new dads. The endorphin release from regular exercise can combat stress and improve mood, making you better equipped to handle the challenges of parenthood. If hitting the gym seems impossible with your new schedule, consider incorporating your baby into your workout routine. Baby-wearing squats, push-ups with your little one on your back, or jogging with a stroller can provide both bonding time and physical activity.

Mindfulness and meditation practices can also be powerful tools for managing stress. Apps like Headspace or Calm offer short, guided meditations that can be done in just a few minutes. You might find that incorporating these practices into your daily routine – perhaps during your baby's nap time or right before bed – helps you stay centered and better able to handle the unpredictability of life with a newborn.

It's also important to maintain social connections outside of your immediate family. While your priorities have shifted, preserving friendships and relationships with extended family can provide valuable support and outlets for stress relief. Schedule regular catch-ups with friends, even if they're just quick video calls or text check-ins. Having a support network beyond your partner can make a world of difference in maintaining your mental health.

Speaking of partners, nurturing your relationship with your significant other is paramount during this period of transition. The arrival of a baby can put immense strain on even the strongest relationships, with 67% of couples reporting a decline in relationship satisfaction during the first three years of their child's life. However, a strong partnership can be your greatest asset in navigating the challenges of parenthood.

Communication becomes more critical than ever during this time. Set aside time each day, even if it's just 10 minutes, to check in with each other about more than just baby-related tasks. Share your feelings, fears, and joys about your new roles. Be honest about your struggles and listen actively to your partner's concerns. Remember, you're in this together, and supporting each other emotionally can strengthen your bond.

Finding time for intimacy and romance might seem like a Herculean task with a new baby, but it's crucial for maintaining your connection as a couple. This doesn't necessarily mean grand gestures or elaborate date nights (though those are great if you can manage them). Small acts of affection – a lingering hug, a heartfelt compliment, or a surprise note of appreciation – can go a long way in keeping the spark alive.

When it comes to physical intimacy, it's important to be patient and understanding. Your partner's body and hormones are still adjusting post-pregnancy, and both of you are likely exhausted. Instead of putting pressure on yourselves to return to your pre-baby sex life immediately, focus on other forms of physical closeness. Cuddling, massage, or simply holding hands while watching a movie can help maintain your physical connection until you're both ready to resume sexual activity.

As your baby grows and becomes more independent, try to schedule regular date nights. These don't have to be elaborate or expensive – a picnic in the park, a movie night at home after the baby is asleep, or a quick coffee date while a family member watches the baby can provide valuable alone time. The key is to make couple time a priority and protect it as fiercely as you would any other important commitment.

Balancing work, family, and personal interests is perhaps one of the most challenging aspects of modern fatherhood. A recent survey found that 48% of working fathers feel they spend too little time with their children, highlighting the struggle many face in juggling their various roles.

One strategy for creating balance is to be fully present in whatever you're doing. When you're at work, focus on your tasks and responsibilities. When you're with your family, put away your phone and give them your undivided attention. This mindful approach can help you feel more fulfilled in each area of your life and reduce the guilt that often comes with feeling pulled in multiple directions.

Technology can be both a blessing and a curse when it comes to work-life balance. While it allows for more flexible working arrangements, it can also blur the lines between work and home life. Set clear boundaries around your work hours and stick to them as much as possible. If you need to work from home, designate a specific workspace and "clock out" at the end of your workday to transition into family time.

Many new fathers find that becoming a parent shifts their priorities and perspective on work. This can be an opportunity to reassess your career goals and ensure they align with your values as a father. Perhaps you'll discover a desire to pursue a more family-friendly work environment or to explore entrepreneurship to have more control over your schedule. Whatever your path, remember that there's no one-size-fits-all solution – the key is finding what works best for you and your family.

Maintaining personal interests and hobbies is vital for your well-being and can actually make you a better father. Engaging in activities you enjoy not only provides stress relief but also helps you maintain a sense of identity beyond your roles as a father and partner. It sets a positive example for your child about the importance of pursuing passions and taking time for oneself.

The trick is to find ways to incorporate your interests into your new lifestyle. If you're a music lover, introduce your baby to your favorite songs during playtime. If you enjoy cooking, involve your little one in meal preparation as they grow older. For activities that require more focused time, consider alternating childcare duties with your partner to ensure you both get opportunities to pursue your interests.

As your child grows, you'll likely find that your personal interests evolve and intertwine with your role as a father. You might discover a newfound passion for coaching youth sports or become an avid collector of children's books. Embrace these changes as part of your journey, and remember that modeling a well-rounded life for your child is one of the greatest gifts you can give them.

It's also important to recognize that your journey as a father will have ups and downs. There will be days when you feel like you're mastering this balancing act, and others when it all seems to fall apart. Be kind to yourself during these times and remember that perfection is not the goal – presence and effort are what truly matter.

Connecting with other fathers can provide valuable support and perspective as you navigate this new chapter of your life. Consider joining a local fathers' group or online community where you can share experiences, seek advice, and find camaraderie with others who understand the unique challenges of modern fatherhood.

As you strive to balance fatherhood with other aspects of your life, remember that this is a continuous process of adjustment and growth. Your needs, your family's needs, and your circumstances will change over time, and so too will your approach to balance. Stay flexible, communicate openly with your partner, and be willing to reassess and adjust your strategies as needed.

Fatherhood is a transformative experience that can bring immense joy, personal growth, and a deep sense of purpose. By prioritizing self-care, nurturing your relationship with your partner, and finding ways to integrate your various roles and interests, you can create a fulfilling life that encompasses both your identity as a father and your individual passions and ambitions.

Remember, there's no perfect formula for balancing fatherhood and your life – it's a personal journey that will look different for every dad. Trust your instincts, be patient with yourself, and savor the incredible moments that come with being a father. The sleepless nights, the career juggling, and the constant balancing act are all part of a grand adventure that will shape you in ways you never imagined.

Keep in mind that your child is watching and learning from you every step of the way. By striving for balance and showing them how to prioritize self-care, relationships, and personal growth alongside family responsibilities, you're teaching invaluable life lessons that will serve them well into adulthood.

Self-Care for Dads: Prioritizing Your Physical and Mental Health.

You've likely heard the flight safety instruction, *"Put on your own oxygen mask before assisting others."* This advice isn't just for air travel—it's a crucial metaphor for fatherhood. Your well-being is the foundation upon which you'll build your family's happiness and health. Yet, in the whirlwind of diaper changes, midnight feedings, and career demands, many dads find themselves at the bottom of their own priority list.

A recent study by the National Institutes of Health found that 70% of new fathers experience increased stress levels in the first year of their child's life. This stress, if left unchecked, can lead to burnout, depression, and even physical health issues. But here's the good news: by implementing some strategic self-care practices, you can not only survive but thrive in your new role.

Let's start with the basics: sleep. Yes, I know what you're thinking. "Sleep? With a newborn? Good luck!" But hear me out. While getting a full eight hours might be a distant dream, there are ways to maximize the sleep you do get. The National Sleep Foundation recommends that adults aim for 7-9 hours of sleep per night. For new dads, this might seem laughable, but it's a goal to work towards.

Try syncing your sleep schedule with your baby's. When they go down for a nap, resist the urge to tackle that pile of dishes or catch up on work emails. Instead, lie down yourself. Even a 20-minute power nap can improve alertness, enhance performance, and reduce mistakes and accidents. A study in the journal Sleep found that a brief nap can even be more effective than caffeine in improving verbal memory, motor skills, and perceptual learning.

Speaking of caffeine, while it might seem like your new best friend, be cautious. Too much can lead to jitters, anxiety, and difficulty sleeping when you do get the chance. Instead, try other energy-boosting strategies. Hydration, for instance, is often overlooked but critically important. Aim for at least 8 glasses of water a day. Dehydration can lead to fatigue, headaches, and difficulty concentrating—all things you don't need when you're already sleep-deprived.

Now, let's talk about nutrition. It's easy to fall into the trap of grabbing whatever's quick and convenient, but fueling your body with nutritious food will pay dividends in energy and overall health. Meal prepping on weekends can be a game-changer. Stock your freezer with healthy, easy-to-heat meals. Smoothies can be a quick way to pack in nutrients—throw in some spinach, fruit,

Greek yogurt, and a scoop of protein powder for a balanced meal you can drink one-handed while holding the baby.

Exercise might seem like a luxury you can't afford, but it's a necessity for both your physical and mental health. A study published in the International Journal of Environmental Research and Public Health found that regular exercise can reduce symptoms of depression and anxiety in new parents. But don't worry, you don't need to hit the gym for hours. Short, high-intensity workouts can be just as effective. Try the *"7-Minute Workout"* app for a quick, full-body routine you can do at home.

Better yet, incorporate your baby into your workout. "Baby wearing" while doing squats or lunges, or using your little one as a weight for chest presses (carefully, of course) can turn bonding time into fitness time. As your child grows, playground workouts can become a fun way to stay active together.

Mental health is just as important as physical health, especially for new dads. A groundbreaking study in the Journal of the American Medical Association found that 10% of new fathers experience postpartum depression. Yet, men are less likely than women to seek help for mental health issues. It's time to change that narrative.

Mindfulness and meditation can be powerful tools for managing stress and improving mental well-being. Apps like Headspace or Calm offer short, guided meditations that you can do in just a few minutes. Try incorporating a brief meditation into your daily routine—perhaps while the baby is napping or right after you put them down for the night.

Journaling is another effective strategy for mental health. It doesn't have to be elaborate—even jotting down three things you're grateful for each day can shift your perspective and improve your mood. A study in the Journal of Personality and

Social Psychology found that practicing gratitude can significantly increase happiness and life satisfaction.

Don't underestimate the power of social connections. While it might be tempting to hibernate with your new family, maintaining friendships and connections with other adults is crucial for your mental health. A study in the Proceedings of the National Academy of Sciences found that social isolation can be as detrimental to health as smoking 15 cigarettes a day.

Consider joining a dad's group or a parenting class. Not only will you meet other fathers going through similar experiences, but you'll also pick up valuable parenting tips. Online forums and social media groups can also provide support and camaraderie, especially during those 3 AM feedings when you feel like the only person awake in the world.

Remember, asking for help is not a sign of weakness—it's a sign of strength and self-awareness. Whether it's talking to a therapist, asking a friend to watch the baby for an hour so you can take a nap, or hiring a cleaner to tackle the housework, accepting help can make a world of difference in your well-being.

Now, let's talk about hobbies. You might think you need to put all your personal interests on hold, but maintaining activities you enjoy is crucial for your identity and mental health. The key is to adapt your hobbies to your new lifestyle. If you're a sports fan, introduce your baby to the game by watching together. If you enjoy reading, try audiobooks during your commute or while doing household chores.

One dad I know, Jude, was an avid rock climber before his daughter was born. He feared he'd have to give up his passion entirely. Instead, he found a climbing gym with childcare services. Now, he climbs for an hour twice a week while his daughter plays in a supervised area. It's become their special outing together, and Jude says those few hours of *"me time"* make him a more patient, energized dad the rest of the week.

Self-care also means setting boundaries. Learn to say no to non-essential commitments that drain your energy. Prioritize activities that truly matter to you and your family. This might mean turning down overtime at work, scaling back on social obligations, or letting go of perfectionist tendencies around the house.

Speaking of the house, create a space that's just for you. It doesn't have to be an entire room—even a comfortable chair in a quiet corner can serve as your sanctuary. Use this space for reading, meditating, or simply sitting quietly for a few minutes each day.

Technology can be both a blessing and a curse for new parents. While it allows us to stay connected and access information easily, it can also be a source of stress and comparison. Implement a "tech curfew" an hour before bed to improve your sleep quality. Use apps like Forest or Freedom to limit your social media usage during the day.

Remember, self-care isn't selfish—it's necessary. By taking care of yourself, you're ensuring that you have the energy, patience, and presence to be the best dad you can be. Think of it as filling your own cup so that you have more to give to your family.

As your child grows, your self-care routine will evolve. What works in the newborn stage might not be feasible with a toddler. Be flexible and willing to adjust your strategies. The important thing is to maintain the mindset that your well-being matters.

My friend, Mark, shared how he struggled with guilt whenever he took time for himself. *"I felt like I should be with my son every free moment I had,"* he said. But after experiencing burnout and snapping at his partner more frequently, He realized something had to change. He started small, taking 15 minutes each evening to go for a walk around the block. *"That little bit of fresh air and solitude made a huge difference,"* he said. *"I came back refreshed and more present for my family."*

Note, you're modeling healthy behaviors for your child. By prioritizing your physical and mental health, you're teaching your little one the importance of self-care from an early age.

As you embark on this self-care journey, be patient with yourself. You won't always get it right, and there will be days when survival mode takes over. That's okay. The goal is progress, not perfection.

Start small. Choose one area to focus on—maybe it's improving your sleep, adding more vegetables to your diet, or setting aside

10 minutes a day for meditation. As these habits become ingrained, you can build on them.

Track your progress. Keep a simple log of your self-care activities and how they make you feel. This can help you identify what works best for you and provide motivation to continue.

Celebrate your wins, no matter how small. Did you drink enough water today? Awesome. Managed a 5-minute workout? Give yourself a high five. These small victories add up to significant changes over time.

Becoming a dad doesn't mean losing yourself. It's about expanding your identity to include this incredible new role. By taking care of yourself, you're not just surviving fatherhood—you're thriving in it. And that's the greatest gift you can give your child and your family.

So, new dad, it's time to put on your oxygen mask. Take a deep breath, and know that by prioritizing your well-being, you're laying the foundation for a happy, healthy family life. You've got this, and you're doing an amazing job.

Maintaining Your Relationship: Nurturing Your Partnership Amidst Parenthood.

The arrival of a baby brings profound joy and excitement, but it also introduces a seismic shift in your relationship with your partner. As you both step into your new roles as parents, it's crucial to remember that you're not just Mom and Dad - you're still partners, lovers, and best friends. Nurturing this core relationship amidst the demands of parenthood is essential for your family's overall happiness and stability.

Research from the Gottman Institute reveals a startling statistic: 67% of couples experience a significant decline in relationship satisfaction within the first three years of their child's life. This doesn't mean your relationship is doomed - far from it. It simply underscores the importance of consciously working on your partnership during this transformative time.

The key is to view your relationship as a living entity that requires regular care and attention, much like your newborn. Just as you wouldn't neglect your baby's needs, you can't afford to put your relationship on autopilot.

Communication becomes more critical than ever during this period. In the sleep-deprived haze of new parenthood, it's easy to let small irritations fester or to assume your partner can read your mind. Make a pact to have regular check-ins with each other, even if it's just for 10 minutes a day. During these moments, put away your phones, look each other in the eye, and really listen.

My neighbors, Jane and Ronald, instituted a nightly "How was your day?" ritual after putting their baby to sleep. "At first, it felt a bit forced," Mike admitted. "But soon, we began to look forward to this time to reconnect and remember that we're more than just parents - we're still us."

Remember, it's not just about talking - it's about how you talk. Dr. John Gottman's research identifies four communication styles that can predict the end of a relationship with 93% accuracy: criticism, contempt, defensiveness, and stonewalling. Be mindful of these in your interactions, especially when you're tired and stressed.

Instead, practice what Gottman calls "gentle start-up." Begin difficult conversations with "I" statements rather than accusatory "you" statements. For example, instead of saying, "You never help with the baby at night," try,

"I'm feeling overwhelmed with the night feedings. Can we brainstorm ways to share this responsibility?"

Physical intimacy often takes a backseat in the early months of parenthood, and that's okay. Your partner's body is still recovering from pregnancy and childbirth, and both of you are likely exhausted. However, it's important not to neglect physical affection entirely.

Small gestures can go a long way in maintaining your physical connection. A lingering hug, a kiss that lasts more than a peck, holding hands while watching TV - these moments of touch can release oxytocin, the "bonding hormone," helping you feel closer even when sex isn't on the table.

When you are ready to resume sexual activity, communication is key. Be open about your desires, fears, and any physical discomfort. Remember, intimacy isn't just about intercourse. Explore other ways to be physically close and bring each other pleasure.

One often overlooked aspect of maintaining your relationship is continuing to have fun together. It's easy to get bogged down in the practicalities of caring for a baby, but don't forget to laugh and play together.

Tom and Lisa, parents of a 6-month-old, found an innovative way to keep the fun alive. "We started having 'living room picnics' after the baby went to sleep," Lisa shared. "We'd spread a blanket on the floor, eat takeout, and play board games. It felt like dating again, even though we couldn't leave the house."

Date nights are important, but they don't have to be elaborate or expensive. A picnic in the backyard while the baby naps, a movie night at home with your favorite snacks, or even doing a puzzle together can provide valuable couple time. The key is to make this time a priority and protect it as fiercely as you would any other important commitment.

As you navigate this new chapter together, it's crucial to maintain a sense of partnership in parenting. Avoid falling into the trap of competitive parenting or keeping score of who does what. Instead, view yourselves as a team working towards the common goal of raising a happy, healthy child.

This teamwork extends to decision-making about your child. Strive to present a united front, even if you disagree behind closed doors. Discuss major parenting decisions together and be willing to compromise. Remember, there's rarely one "right" way to parent, and your child will benefit from exposure to both of your parenting styles.

Support each other's relationship with the baby. Encourage your partner to have one-on-one time with the child, and resist the urge to swoop in and "fix" things if they're struggling. This not only strengthens their bond with the baby but also gives you a much-needed break.

Maintaining individual identities within your partnership is also crucial. Encourage each other to pursue personal interests and maintain friendships outside of your relationship. This not only provides a sense of fulfillment but also brings fresh energy and experiences back into your partnership.

James and Maria made a pact to give each other regular "me time." "Every Saturday, I take the baby for the morning so Maria can go to her art class," James explained. "And on Sundays, she does the same for me so I can play basketball with my friends. It makes us both better parents and partners when we return."

Remember to express appreciation for each other regularly. In the daily grind of parenthood, it's easy to focus on what isn't getting done rather than acknowledging each other's efforts. Make it a habit to thank your partner for specific things they do, no matter how small.

A study in the Journal of Personality and Social Psychology found that feeling appreciated by your partner is one of the strongest predictors of relationship satisfaction. So, whether it's for changing a diaper, making dinner, or simply being a listening ear after a tough day, express your gratitude often.

It's also important to maintain a sense of romance in your relationship. This doesn't mean grand gestures or expensive gifts - small, thoughtful acts can be just as meaningful. Leave a loving note in your partner's lunch bag, send a flirty text during the day, or surprise them with their favorite treat.

Alex, shared how he keeps the romance alive: "Every week, I try to do one small thing to make my wife smile. Sometimes it's as simple as drawing a heart on the bathroom mirror with her lipstick or setting up a candlelit bath for her after a long day. It's not much, but it reminds her that she's still the love of my life, not just the mother of my child."

As you focus on your relationship, don't forget to be kind to yourselves and each other. The transition to parenthood is challenging, and you'll both make mistakes along the way. Practice forgiveness - both for your partner and yourself. Remember that you're both learning and growing in your new roles.

Lastly, don't be afraid to seek help if you're struggling. Many couples find that the transition to parenthood brings up unexpected issues or exacerbates existing ones. Couples therapy isn't a sign of failure - it's a proactive step towards strengthening your relationship. A skilled therapist can provide tools and strategies to help you communicate more effectively and navigate this new chapter together.

Maintaining your relationship amidst the demands of parenthood is no small feat, but it's one of the most important things you can do for your family. A strong partnership provides a stable foundation for your child to grow and thrive. By prioritizing your relationship, communicating openly, maintaining physical and emotional intimacy, and supporting each other's growth, you're not just surviving parenthood - you're creating a loving, joyful family environment that will benefit your child for years to come.

Chapter 12

Embracing the Joy of Fatherhood

"Being a father has been, without a doubt, my greatest source of achievement, pride, and inspiration. Fatherhood has taught me about unconditional love, reinforced the importance of giving back, and taught me how to be a better person." - Naveen Jain

As you approach the end of your baby's first year, you might find yourself in a reflective mood. The sleepless nights, diaper changes, and seemingly endless crying sessions have given way to something truly remarkable - you've become a father. This transformation, while often challenging, is also profoundly rewarding. Let's explore the joys and unique experiences that make fatherhood an incomparable journey.

The moment you first held your child, you likely experienced a rush of emotions unlike anything you'd felt before. That instant connection, the overwhelming sense of protection and love, is just the beginning of the fatherhood experience. As your child grows, you'll find that these feelings deepen and evolve in ways you never imagined possible.

One of the most magical aspects of fatherhood is witnessing your child's firsts. From their first smile to their first steps, these milestones are etched into your memory forever. There's an indescribable pride in seeing your little one achieve something new, knowing that you played a part in their development. The first time your baby recognizes you and reaches out for you specifically is a moment of pure joy that many fathers describe as life-changing.

But it's not just the big moments that make fatherhood special. It's the everyday experiences that build the foundation of your relationship with your child. The quiet moments of rocking your baby to sleep, the silly faces you make to elicit a giggle, or the way your child's hand feels in yours as you walk together - these are the building blocks of a bond that will last a lifetime.

Fatherhood also offers a unique opportunity for personal growth. Many men find that becoming a father pushes them to be better versions of themselves. You might discover reserves of patience you never knew you had, or find yourself more empathetic and understanding. The responsibility of raising a child often leads to increased motivation in other areas of life, as you strive to provide the best possible future for your family.

Reflect on how you've changed since becoming a father. Perhaps you've become more organized, learning to juggle the demands of work and family life. Maybe you've developed a new appreciation for your own parents, understanding for the first time the depth of their love and sacrifice. You might have found a new sense of purpose, with your child's wellbeing becoming your primary motivation in life decisions.

Many fathers report a shift in their priorities and values after having a child. Things that once seemed important may now pale in comparison to your family's happiness and security. This realignment can lead to positive changes in various aspects of your life, from career choices to personal habits.

The journey of fatherhood is also one of continuous learning. Your child becomes your greatest teacher, showing you the world through fresh eyes. You'll rediscover the joy of simple pleasures, like the excitement of a butterfly sighting or the wonder of a colorful sunset. Your child's curiosity can reignite your own, leading to shared adventures and discoveries.

As your child grows, you'll find that fatherhood continues to evolve. Each stage brings new joys and challenges. The toddler years, while often trying, are filled with adorable moments as your child's personality begins to shine through. You'll delight in their imaginative play, their budding sense of humor, and their insatiable curiosity about the world around them.

The school years bring a different kind of satisfaction. Watching your child learn to read, make friends, and develop their own interests is deeply rewarding. You'll have the opportunity to be their guide, helping them navigate social situations and academic challenges. The pride you feel when your child succeeds - whether it's in a school play, a sports event, or simply mastering a new skill - is unparalleled.

As your child enters adolescence, your role will shift again. While this period can be challenging, it also offers unique opportunities for connection. You'll have the chance to engage in deeper conversations, sharing your values and experiences. Watching your child develop their own identity and start to make their way in the world is both exciting and bittersweet.

Throughout all these stages, one of the greatest joys of fatherhood is the unconditional love you share with your child. This love transforms you, making you more vulnerable but also infinitely stronger. It's a love that motivates you to be your best self, to overcome obstacles, and to face each day with renewed purpose.

Fatherhood also offers the chance to create and pass on family traditions. Whether it's a special birthday ritual, a holiday tradition, or simply a regular family game night, these shared experiences create lasting memories and strengthen family bonds. As you establish these traditions, you're not just creating fun moments - you're building your family's unique culture and identity.

Many fathers find that having a child deepens their connection to their community and the world at large. You might find yourself more invested in local issues, particularly those affecting children and families. Some fathers become advocates for causes they care about, wanting to create a better world for their children to inherit. This expanded sense of responsibility and connection can be deeply fulfilling.

The role of fathers in child development has been increasingly recognized in recent years. Research has shown that involved fathers have a significant positive impact on their children's cognitive abilities, educational achievement, psychological well-being, and social behavior. Knowing that your involvement is crucial to your child's development can be both empowering and motivating.

One study published in the Journal of Marriage and Family found that children with involved fathers are 43% more likely to earn A's in school and 33% less likely to repeat a grade than those without involved dads. Another study from the University of Oxford found that children whose fathers were highly involved in their upbringing had fewer behavioral problems and higher IQ test scores.

These findings underscore the importance of your role as a father and can serve as encouragement during challenging times. Every bedtime story you read, every scraped knee you bandage, and every words of encouragement you offer are contributing to your child's long-term success and well-being.

Fatherhood also offers a unique opportunity for self-reflection and personal growth. As you guide your child through life's challenges, you may find yourself reconsidering your own values, beliefs, and behaviors. Many fathers report that having a child made them more aware of their own strengths and weaknesses, spurring personal development.

You might discover new aspects of your personality - a playfulness you didn't know you possessed, or a well of patience you never realized you had. You may find yourself becoming more emotionally expressive, as you learn to communicate with your child on their level. This emotional growth can have positive ripple effects in other areas of your life, improving your relationships with your partner, friends, and colleagues.

The journey of fatherhood is also one of constant adaptation. As your child grows and changes, so too must your parenting style. This need for flexibility can be challenging, but it's also an opportunity for continuous growth and learning. You'll develop problem-solving skills, learn to think on your feet, and become more adaptable - all valuable skills in every aspect of life.

One of the most profound joys of fatherhood is the opportunity to shape a young life. Your words, actions, and attitudes will play a crucial role in forming your child's worldview and character. This responsibility can feel daunting at times, but it's also incredibly rewarding. Seeing your child embody the values you've tried to instill - kindness, honesty, perseverance - is deeply satisfying.

As your child grows, you'll have the chance to share your passions and interests with them. Whether it's a love of sports, music, nature, or any other pursuit, introducing your child to the things that bring you joy can be a wonderful bonding experience. You might rediscover old hobbies through your child's eyes or find new shared interests to explore together.

Fatherhood also offers endless opportunities for laughter and fun. Children have a unique ability to find joy in the simplest things, and their laughter is contagious. From silly games and dad jokes to family adventures and playful roughhousing, the moments of pure joy and laughter you share with your child are priceless.

Many fathers report that having a child has made them more aware of the passage of time. While this can sometimes feel bittersweet, it also encourages you to be more present and to cherish each moment. You become acutely aware that your child won't be small forever, which can motivate you to make the most of each stage of their childhood.

As you look to the future, there's so much to anticipate. You have a lifetime of experiences ahead - teaching your child to ride a bike, cheering them on at sports events or recitals, having deep conversations about life, celebrating their achievements, and supporting them through challenges. While the nature of your relationship will change as your child grows, the bond you're building now will last a lifetime.

Fatherhood is a journey that continues long after your child has grown. Even when your child becomes an adult, you'll always be their father. The relationship will evolve, potentially becoming more of a friendship, but the foundation of love and support you're building now will always be there.

Many fathers find that one of the greatest joys of parenthood is seeing their child become a parent themselves. Watching your child navigate the challenges and joys of raising their own children can be a profoundly moving experience. You'll have the opportunity to offer guidance and support, drawing on your own experiences as a father.

It's okay to find it challenging at times. The sleepless nights, the worries, the moments of frustration - these are all part of the journey. But they're balanced by moments of indescribable joy, deep connection, and immense pride.

Fatherhood is a role that will challenge you, change you, and ultimately fulfill you in ways you never imagined possible. It's a lifelong adventure filled with love, learning, and growth. As you continue on this journey, remember to cherish each moment, celebrate the small victories, and most importantly, enjoy the incredible privilege of being a dad.

Your child's first year is just the beginning. The adventure of fatherhood stretches out before you, filled with promise and possibility. Embrace it with an open heart, a sense of wonder, and the knowledge that you're embarking on the most important and rewarding role of your life. The journey of fatherhood is one of constant discovery - about your child, about the world, and about yourself. It's a journey that will transform you, challenge you, and ultimately bring you joy beyond measure.

Celebrating Your Achievements: Recognizing Your Growth as a Father.

As you approach the end of your baby's first year, it's time to pause and reflect on the incredible journey you've undertaken. Becoming a father is no small feat, and the growth you've experienced in this role deserves recognition. Let's take a moment to celebrate your achievements and acknowledge the remarkable transformation you've undergone.

Think back to the day you first learned you were going to be a dad. Perhaps you felt a mix of excitement and trepidation, wondering if you were truly ready for this monumental change in your life. Now, as you look at your thriving one-year-old, you can see tangible proof of your success. You've not only kept this tiny human alive but helped them flourish and grow into a unique individual with their own personality.

One of the most significant achievements to recognize is your ability to adapt. Fatherhood has likely thrown you curveballs you never expected. From mastering the art of diaper changes at 3 AM to deciphering your baby's cries, you've developed a new set of skills that you probably never imagined you'd need. This adaptability is a testament to your resilience and commitment to your role as a father.

Consider how your priorities have shifted over the past year. Where once your focus might have been primarily on your career or personal interests, you've learned to balance these with the needs of your family. This reprioritization is no small feat. It requires emotional maturity and a willingness to put others' needs before your own – qualities that mark you as a dedicated father.

Your emotional growth is another area worthy of celebration. Many men find that fatherhood opens up new depths of feeling they hadn't previously explored. You've likely experienced a range of emotions, from overwhelming love to frustration and everything in between. Your ability to navigate these feelings, to be vulnerable with your child and partner, and to express your emotions in healthy ways is a significant achievement.

Recall the first time you successfully soothed your crying baby or got them to laugh. These moments, while seemingly small, represent major victories in your journey as a father. They demonstrate your growing ability to connect with your child, to understand their needs, and to provide comfort and joy. This emotional attunement is a skill that will serve you well throughout your child's life.

You've also likely grown in your capacity for patience. The constant demands of a baby can test even the calmest individual, but you've risen to the challenge. Whether it's enduring sleepless nights, dealing with feeding struggles, or simply learning to slow down to match your baby's pace, you've cultivated a level of patience that will benefit you in all areas of life.

Your problem-solving skills have undoubtedly sharpened over the past year. Parenthood presents a constant stream of challenges, from figuring out the best way to babyproof your home to determining why your little one suddenly refuses to eat their favorite food. Each problem you've solved has built your confidence and resourcefulness as a father.

Consider how your relationship skills have evolved. Becoming a parent often puts strain on a partnership, but you've worked to maintain a strong connection with your partner while taking on your new role. You've learned to communicate more effectively, to share responsibilities, and to support each other through the ups and downs of new parenthood. This growth in your relationship skills is a significant achievement that will benefit your entire family.

Your physical stamina and dexterity have likely improved as well. From carrying a growing baby to assembling nursery furniture and chasing after a crawling infant, fatherhood is a physical job. You've probably discovered strength and energy reserves you didn't know you had. Celebrate this physical resilience – it's preparing you for the active years of toddlerhood ahead!

Reflect on how your worldview has expanded since becoming a father. You may find that you're more aware of social issues, more concerned about the future of the planet, or more invested in your local community. This broadened perspective is a form of personal growth that can lead to positive changes not just for your family, but for society as a whole.

Your ability to multitask has undoubtedly improved. You've learned to juggle work responsibilities with diaper changes, to cook dinner while entertaining a baby, and perhaps even to type one-handed while holding a sleeping infant. This improved efficiency and ability to handle multiple demands simultaneously is a valuable skill that will serve you well in all aspects of life.

Consider the wealth of knowledge you've accumulated over the past year. You've become an expert on your baby's needs, preferences, and developmental milestones. You've educated yourself on everything from safe sleep practices to introducing solid foods. This commitment to learning and growing for the sake of your child is commendable.

Your capacity for selflessness has grown immensely. You've likely sacrificed sleep, personal time, and perhaps even career opportunities for the sake of your family. While it's important to maintain a balance and take care of yourself, this willingness to put your child's needs first is a hallmark of great fatherhood.

Reflect on how you've become more present and mindful. The fast pace of modern life often makes it challenging to live in the moment, but caring for a baby requires a level of presence that can be transformative. You've learned to fully engage with your child, to notice small changes in their development, and to find joy in simple moments. This increased mindfulness is a valuable personal growth that can enhance all areas of your life.

Your decision-making skills have likely been honed over the past year. From choosing the right childcare option to making medical decisions for your baby, you've had to weigh options carefully and make choices that impact your whole family. This improved decision-making ability is an important aspect of personal growth that will serve you well as a father and in your professional life.

Consider how your time management skills have evolved. With a baby in the picture, time becomes a precious commodity. You've learned to maximize productivity during nap times, to streamline your routines, and to prioritize what's truly important. This improved efficiency is a valuable skill that can benefit all aspects of your life.

Your empathy and compassion have likely grown as well. Caring for a helpless infant naturally increases one's capacity for understanding and compassion. You may find that you're more patient with others, more understanding of different perspectives, and more inclined to help those in need. This emotional growth not only makes you a better father but a better person overall.

Celebrate the ways in which you've become a role model. Whether you realize it or not, your child has been watching and learning from you since day one. By showing up consistently, expressing love openly, and demonstrating positive behaviors, you're setting a powerful example for your child. This responsibility to be a role model can be a significant motivator for personal growth and positive change.

Acknowledge the courage you've shown in embracing this new role. Becoming a father requires a leap of faith. You've faced fears, taken on new responsibilities, and ventured into unknown territory. This willingness to embrace change and challenge yourself is a testament to your personal growth and strength of character.

Your ability to find humor in challenging situations has likely improved. Parenthood is full of moments that could be frustrating if you don't learn to laugh at them. Whether it's a diaper blowout at an inopportune moment or a messy feeding attempt, your ability to find the humor in these situations is a valuable coping skill and a sign of emotional maturity.

Recognize how you've grown in your ability to ask for and accept help. Many men struggle with this, but fatherhood often necessitates reaching out to others for support and advice. Learning to build a support network and accept assistance when needed is a significant personal growth that will serve you well throughout your parenting journey.

As you reflect on these areas of growth and achievement, take a moment to feel proud of how far you've come. The man you were a year ago has evolved into a capable, loving father. This growth didn't happen overnight — it's the result of countless moments of challenge, joy, frustration, and love.

The journey of fatherhood is ongoing, and there will always be new challenges to face and new opportunities for growth. But for now, pause and celebrate the father you've become. You've navigated the uncharted waters of your baby's first year with grace, humor, and love. That's an achievement worth recognizing.

Your growth as a father is a gift not only to your child but to yourself and your entire family. The patience, empathy, resilience, and love you've cultivated will continue to shape your journey as a father and as a man. So here's to you, dad – to the sleepless nights you've endured, the skills you've mastered, the love you've given, and the incredible growth you've achieved. You're doing an amazing job, and the best is yet to come.

Looking Ahead: Embracing the Lifelong Journey of Parenthood

As you close this book and reflect on the incredible journey you've embarked upon, remember that fatherhood is not just about surviving the first year - it's a lifelong adventure that will continually shape and redefine you. The skills you've honed, the patience you've developed, and the love you've nurtured during this initial phase are just the foundation for the years to come.

Looking ahead, you'll find that each stage of your child's life brings its own unique joys and challenges. The toddler years will test your reflexes as you chase after a newly mobile explorer, while simultaneously melting your heart with their first words and the pure, unfiltered love they show you. You'll become a master of "dad reflexes," catching falling objects and wobbling toddlers with superhuman speed.

As your child enters preschool and elementary school, you'll witness their personality blossoming in new ways. You'll be their first and most important teacher, guiding them through life's early lessons. From tying shoelaces to riding a bike, you'll be there to celebrate every milestone. Your role will evolve from caregiver to coach, cheerleader, and confidant.

A study by the National Center for Education Statistics found that children whose fathers are involved in their schooling are more likely to get A's and enjoy school. Your engagement in their education - helping with homework, attending school events, and fostering a love of learning - will have a lasting impact on their academic success and overall attitude towards knowledge.

The preteen and teenage years will bring a new set of adventures. You'll navigate the complex waters of adolescence together, helping your child build self-esteem, make good decisions, and develop their own identity. While these years can be challenging, they also offer opportunities for deeper connections and meaningful conversations. Your guidance during this time will be crucial in shaping the adult your child will become.

Research from the Journal of Youth and Adolescence shows that teens who have a close, supportive relationship with their fathers are more likely to have higher self-esteem and better mental health. Your presence and involvement during these formative years can make a significant difference in your child's life trajectory.

As they grow into adulthood, your relationship will continue to evolve. You'll transition from being an authority figure to more of a mentor and friend. You'll share in their triumphs, offer comfort during setbacks, and perhaps even welcome grandchildren into the family. The bond you've built will serve as a foundation for a lifelong friendship.

Throughout this journey, you'll find that fatherhood continues to change you in unexpected ways. You might discover new strengths, develop hidden talents, or find yourself passionate about causes that affect children and families. Many fathers report that having children made them more empathetic, patient, and socially conscious.

A longitudinal study published in the Journal of Marriage and Family found that men who become fathers experience significant personality changes. They tend to become more conscientious and emotionally stable, with these positive changes persisting well into their children's adolescence and beyond.

Your influence as a father extends far beyond your immediate family. By raising a kind, compassionate, and responsible child, you're contributing to a better society. Your actions and attitudes will shape not only your child but potentially generations to come.

Consider the legacy you want to leave as a father. What values do you want to instill? What family traditions do you want to create or continue? How do you want your child to remember their childhood and their relationship with you? These are powerful questions to reflect on as you continue your fatherhood journey.

One of the most rewarding aspects of long-term fatherhood is seeing your child develop their own passions and pursuits. You might find yourself learning about dinosaurs, space exploration, or ballet as you support their interests. Embrace these opportunities to see the world through your child's eyes and to learn alongside them.

As your child grows, you'll also have the chance to share your own passions and skills. Whether it's teaching them to fish, cook, play an instrument, or work on cars, these shared experiences will create lasting memories and strengthen your bond. Don't underestimate the impact of these moments - they're often the ones children cherish most as they grow older.

Remember, too, that fatherhood is not a solo journey. As you move forward, continue to nurture your relationship with your partner. Your strong partnership will provide a stable foundation for your child's growth and development. Make time for date nights, open communication, and mutual support. A happy, healthy relationship between parents is one of the greatest gifts you can give your child.

In the years to come, you'll face challenges you can't yet imagine. From helping your child navigate their first heartbreak to supporting them as they make major life decisions, your role will be crucial. Trust in the foundation you've built during this first year, and know that you have the strength and wisdom to guide your child through whatever life brings.

Don't forget to take care of yourself along the way. Self-care isn't selfish - it's essential for being the best father you can be. Continue to pursue your own interests, maintain friendships, and prioritize your physical and mental health. Model work-life balance for your child, showing them that it's possible to be a devoted parent while also nurturing other aspects of life.

Stay curious and open to learning. Your child will teach you as much as you teach them. They'll challenge your assumptions, broaden your perspectives, and push you to grow in ways you never expected. Welcome these opportunities for personal development.

Looking ahead, you might feel a mix of excitement and apprehension. That's normal and, in fact, a sign of how seriously you take this role. But remember, you've already conquered one of the most challenging phases - the first year. You've proven your resilience, adaptability, and capacity for love. These qualities will serve you well in the years to come.

Fatherhood is a journey without a final destination. Each stage brings new joys, challenges, and opportunities for growth. Embrace the uncertainty, celebrate the victories (both big and small), and know that every day, you're making a difference in your child's life.

As this book comes to a close, know that you're well-equipped for the adventure ahead. You've gained knowledge, developed skills, and most importantly, opened your heart to the transformative power of fatherhood. Trust in yourself, in the bond you've formed with your child, and in the love that will guide you through the years to come.

Remember the words of author Kent Nerburn: "It is not flesh and blood, but the heart which makes us fathers and sons." The love you've cultivated, the memories you've created, and the lessons you've shared will form the heart of your relationship with your child for years to come.

As you step forward into the next phase of fatherhood, carry with you the wonder of those first moments holding your newborn, the triumph of surviving sleepless nights, and the joy of witnessing your baby's first smile. These experiences have laid the groundwork for a lifetime of love, growth, and connection.

Your journey as a father is uniquely yours. There will be moments of doubt, times of struggle, and days when you feel overwhelmed. But there will also be moments of pure joy, times of incredible pride, and days when your heart feels so full it might burst. Embrace it all. Each experience, whether challenging or rewarding, is shaping you into the father your child needs.

As you close this book, know that you're not just ending a chapter - you're beginning a lifelong story of love, growth, and adventure. The title of "Dad" is one you'll carry proudly for the rest of your life. It's a role that will challenge you, change you, and ultimately fulfill you in ways you never imagined possible.

So here's to you, new dad. To the sleepless nights you've endured, the diapers you've changed, the lullabies you've sung. To the father you are and the father you're becoming. The adventure of a lifetime awaits. Embrace it with an open heart, a curious mind, and the knowledge that you're embarking on the most important and rewarding role of your life.

The journey ahead is filled with promise and possibility. You've got this, Dad. Now go out there and embrace the incredible adventure of fatherhood.

Dear Reader,

Thank you for embarking on this incredible journey with me through the pages of "I Am Going to be a Dad." Your decision to pick up this book and invest your time in preparing for fatherhood means the world to me. I hope that as you've read, you've found not just information, but also reassurance, encouragement, and maybe even a few laughs along the way.

Writing this book has been a labor of love, fueled by my own experiences as a father and the desire to support other men as they step into this life-changing role. Your trust in this guide truly humbles me.

As you close this book and continue on your path to fatherhood, remember that you're not alone. You're part of a community of dads who are redefining what it means to be a father in the modern world. Your journey is unique, but the challenges, joys, and transformations you'll experience

264

connect you to countless other fathers out there.

If you found value in these pages, I'd be incredibly grateful if you could take a moment to leave an honest review. Your feedback not only helps other dads-to-be find this resource but also contributes to the ongoing conversation about modern fatherhood. Your insights and experiences can make a real difference for future readers who, like you, are looking for guidance as they prepare to become dads.

Thank you again for allowing me to be a small part of your fatherhood journey. Remember, you've got this! Wishing you all the best as you embrace the adventure of a lifetime.

With gratitude and best wishes for your fatherhood journey,

Mike Fatherman